Let's Read Aloud & Learn English:
On Campus

音読で学ぶ基礎英語≪キャンパス編≫

By
Teruhiko Kadoyama
&
Simon Capper

 SEIBIDO

photographs by

iStockphoto

Let's Read Aloud & Learn English: On Campus

はしがき

　本書は、「音読」や「筆写」といった、一見地味ですが確実に英語力アップにつながる練習法を取り入れた総合英語テキストで、『音読で始める基礎英語』シリーズの第 3 弾に当たるものです。前 2 作同様、基礎的な語彙や文法の確認に重点を置いていますが、本作はキャンパスライフを舞台にしたストーリー仕立てになっていますので、アルバイトや期末試験など、日々の生活の中で密着した表現を数多く学ぶことができるはずです。

　「英語をペラペラ話せるようになりたい」と願う人は多いですが、授業や自宅での学習で実際にどれだけ英語を音読する練習をしてきたでしょうか？　何度も音読しなければやはり英語が口からすぐに出てくるようにはなりませんし、実際に英文を書いてみるという作業は表現を確認し定着させる上で非常に効果的です。デジタル全盛な時代にあえてこうしたアナログ的な練習方法を提唱するのは、やはり一番効果が実感しやすい方法だと思うからです。

　しかし、本書はアナログ的な面だけを重視したテキストでは決してありません。本書は Web 英語学習システムの LINGUAPORTA（リンガポルタ）に対応していますので、パソコンやスマートフォンを使ったモバイル・ラーニングが可能です。アナログとデジタルのそれぞれ良い点を皆さんの英語学習に活かしてほしいと願っています。

　本書は 15 ユニットからなり、各ユニットの構成は次のようになっています。

■ **WARM-UP**：授業で聞く対話の中に出てくる重要単語や表現、そして文法項目を取り上げていますので、あらかじめ確認しておくと聞き取りが易しく感じられるはずです。ここは授業の予習としてやっておきましょう。

■ **LET'S LISTEN!**：キャンパスライフを舞台にした対話を聞いてみましょう。対話の大意が理解できているかを試す問題が用意されています。

■ **LET'S CHECK & READ ALOUD!**：空欄補充問題を設けていますので、LET'S LISTEN! で聞いた対話をもう 1 度聞いて空欄を埋めてみましょう。内容を確認したら、音読、そしてパートナーとロールプレイ（役割練習）をしてみましょう。QR コードからアクセスできるオンライン動画を用意していますので、ぜひ自宅学習でも積極的に取り入れてください。そうすればその効果が実感できることでしょう。

■ **GRAMMAR**：WARM-UP で取り上げた文法項目の確認問題です。文法に苦手意識のある方はこのページでしっかり復習をしておきましょう。

■ **LET'S READ!**：英米の大学や異文化理解に関するパッセージを読んでみましょう。大意が理解できているかを試す問題が用意されています。

■ **CHALLENGE YOURSELF!**：英語の資格試験としてよく知られている TOEIC Bridge® と似た形式のリスニング問題を用意しました。試験を意識した実践的な演習をしてみましょう。

■ **LET'S READ ALOUD & WRITE!**：最後に授業のまとめとして、学習した対話を音読筆写してみましょう。日本語訳だけを見ながら英文がスラスラと書けるようになることが目標です。

　本書の刊行にあたっては、成美堂の佐野英一郎氏、そして編集部の工藤隆志氏、萩原美奈子氏に多大なご尽力を賜りました。衷心よりお礼申し上げます。

角山照彦
Simon Capper

● Table of Contents

主な登場人物

Takashi

心理学を専攻する大学１年生

Cathy

タカシの英語の先生
（イギリス人）

Martha

アメリカからの留学生

Jenny

イギリスからの留学生

What's your major?

be 動詞

タカシは学生食堂でキャシー先生に話しかけます。会話では、話しかけたり、自己紹介したりする際の表現を学びます。また、文法では **be 動詞**（現在形・過去形）と疑問詞に焦点を当てて学習します。

 WARM-UP　　　　　　　　　授業前に確認しておこう！

Vocabulary Preview

1 〜 10 の語句の意味として適切なものを a 〜 j の中から選びましょう。　　🎧 02

1. cafeteria	＿＿＿＿	a. うれしくて
2. crowded	＿＿＿＿	b. 興味深い、面白い
3. go ahead	＿＿＿＿	c.（人から聞いた情報などが）〜に聞こえる
4. glad	＿＿＿＿	d. 1 年生
5. freshman	＿＿＿＿	e. 心理学
6. major	＿＿＿＿	f.（命令文で）さあどうぞ
7. seat	＿＿＿＿	g. セルフサービス式の食堂
8. psychology	＿＿＿＿	h.（大学の）専攻
9. sound	＿＿＿＿	i. 座席
10. interesting	＿＿＿＿	j. 混雑した

ビートに乗って 1 〜 10 の語句を発音してみましょう。

Grammar Point be 動詞

I'm a freshman, and my major is law. （私は大学 1 年生で、専攻は法律です）
I was a member of the tennis club in high school.

（高校の時はテニス部に所属していました）

be 動詞とは名詞や形容詞、場所を表す語句が後に続いて「〜である、〜にいる」という意味を表すもので、主語によっていろいろと形が変わります。また、「〜だった、〜にいた」と過去を表す場合も同じく変化します。下の表の空欄に枠の中から適切な動詞の形を選んで表を完成させましょう。

> was
> am ✓
> is
> are
> were

主 語			現在形	過去形
1人称	単数（私）	I	*am*	
	複数（私たち）	we		
2人称	単数（あなた）	you		
	複数（あなたたち）			
3人称	単数（彼、彼女、それ）	he, she, it		
	複数（彼ら、それら）	they		

話し手のことを
1 人称、
相手方を **2 人称**、
それ以外の人たちを
3 人称と言います。

「〜ではない」という否定文にするときは、be 動詞のすぐ後に not をつけます。また、「〜ですか？」という疑問文にするには be 動詞を主語の前に持ってきます。下の例文の日本語訳を完成させながら確認しましょう。

The cafeteria <u>isn't</u> crowded after one o'clock.

（ ＿＿＿＿＿＿＿＿＿＿＿＿＿＿＿＿＿＿＿＿＿＿＿ ）

<u>Is</u> the cafeteria very crowded now?

（ ＿＿＿＿＿＿＿＿＿＿＿＿＿＿＿＿＿＿＿＿＿＿＿ ）

　なお、疑問文を作る際には、when や where などの**疑問詞**がよく使われますが、これらは通常疑問文の始めに置かれます。下の表で確認した後、例文の日本語訳を完成させましょう。

what	何	who	誰	how	どのように
where	どこへ（で）	why	なぜ	how far	どれくらいの距離
when	いつ	which	どれ	how long	どれくらいの時間

"My major is education. <u>What's</u> yours?" "It's psychology."

（ ＿＿＿＿＿＿＿＿＿＿＿＿＿＿＿＿＿＿＿＿＿＿＿＿＿ ）

"<u>How far</u> is it from here to your apartment?" "It's only a five-minute walk from here."

（ ＿＿＿＿＿＿＿＿＿＿＿＿＿＿＿＿＿＿＿＿＿＿＿＿＿ ）

　be 動詞は、単に「（〜は）…である」と言う場合だけでなく、《be going to ...》の形で未来形、《be ＋ -ing》の形で進行形、《be ＋過去分詞》の形で受動態など、様々な表現で使われます。基本をしっかりと確認しておきましょう。

 ## LET'S LISTEN!　　　　　　　　　会話の大意を聞き取ろう！

タカシとキャシー先生の会話を聞いて、質問に対する答えとして最も適切なものを A 〜 C の中から１つ選びましょう。　 03

Question 1　Is the cafeteria crowded now?

　A. Yes, it's always crowded.
　B. No, it's not so crowded.
　C. No, it's not crowded at all.

Question 2　Is this the first time for Takashi to meet Ms. Baker?

　A. Yes, it is.
　B. No, he was in her class last year.
　C. No, he was in her class this morning.

Question 3　What does Ms. Baker ask Takashi?

　A. His hometown
　B. His main course of study
　C. His club activity

LET'S CHECK & READ ALOUD!　音読してみよう！

1. スクリプトを見ながら会話をもう１度聞き、下線部に当てはまる表現を書き入れましょう。（下線部には単語が２つ入ります）
2. 内容を確認して、全文を音読してみましょう。
3. タカシとキャシー先生の役割をパートナーと一緒に演じてみましょう。

 03

Let's Practice the Roleplay!

Takashi's Role　Cathy's Role

最後にQRコードから動画にアクセスして各自ロールプレイの練習をしましょう。

Takashi speaks to Ms. Baker at the school cafeteria.

Takashi　Excuse me. Is ① _____ taken?

Cathy　No, go ahead.

Takashi　Thank you. This cafeteria ② _____ crowded.

Cathy　Yes. It's very crowded.

Takashi　I ③ _____ your class this morning, Ms. Baker. It was very interesting.

Cathy　Oh, ④ _____ to hear that. Just call me Cathy.

Takashi　All right, Cathy. By the way, I'm Takashi Kudo. Please call me Takashi.

Cathy　OK, Takashi. So, you're ⑤ _____, right?

Takashi　Yes, ⑥ _____.

Cathy　⑦ _____ major?

Takashi　Psychology.

Cathy　⑧ _____.

♪ 音読のヒント ♪

seat など、カタカナ英語として定着している単語は、「シート」のように「スィ」（[si]）を「シ」（[ʃi]）と読んでしまいがちですが、正しく「スィート」[síːt] と発音するようにしましょう。また、ワークシートなどに使われる sheet は、カタカナ英語に近く「シート」[ʃíːt] と発音されます。
同様に、she と see も、それぞれ「シー」[ʃíː]、「スィー」[síː] と正しく発音しましょう。

 **GRAMMAR**

A. 例にならい、カッコ内に適切な be 動詞を書き入れましょう。

> 例　Martha (　*is*　) from Ohio.

1. These bags (　　　　　) heavy. Can you help me?
2. I feel fine today, but I (　　　　　) sick last night.
3. My brother (　　　　　) sick, but he's better now.
4. We (　　　　　) in London this time last year.

B. 例にならい、A と B の対話が成り立つように枠の中から適切な疑問詞を選んで文を完成させましょう。

> 例　A: ___Where's___ Martha from?
>　　　B: Ohio.

1. A: _____ your birthday?

   B: July 21.
2. A: _____ the woman in this picture?

   B: Ms. Baker. She's my English teacher.
3. A: _____ you late this morning?

   B: I missed the train.
4. A: May I help you?

   B: These shoes are nice. _____ they?

   A: Seventy dollars.

> what
> when
> who
> where ✓
> why
> which
> how
> how much
> how far

C. 日本語の意味に合うようにカッコ内の語句を並べ替え、英文を完成させましょう。ただし、文の始めにくる単語も小文字にしてあり、1 つ余分な語句が含まれています。

1. この近くに病院はありますか？

   (is / a hospital / here / there / near / are)?

   _____
2. どうして学校に遅刻したのですか？

   (late / were / was / for / why / you) school?

   _____
3. このプリンターはどこかおかしいです。

   (are / wrong / with / this / is / something) printer.

   _____
4. 食堂はあまり混んでいませんでした。

   (crowded / were / the cafeteria / was / not / very).

   _____

次のパッセージを読んで１〜３の質問に答えましょう。 04

What? No Entrance Ceremonies?

Have you ever seen a university graduation ceremony in a Hollywood movie? In a movie, students look happy in their <u>gowns</u> and throw their hats into the air with joy. It's a scene that happens across the U.S. every year. But have you ever wondered why there are never any scenes of entrance ceremonies? It's because in American and British universities, there are no entrance ceremonies. It's difficult to know why this important stage in life isn't celebrated. Perhaps because traditionally, in the U.S. and Britain, it's been easier to get into university, but harder to graduate than in Japan.

1. Scenes of _____ are often seen in a Hollywood movie.

   A. university entrance ceremonies

   B. university graduation ceremonies

   C. university entrance examinations

2. The underlined word "gowns" means loose-fitting items of clothing that are often worn at _____.

   A. formal ceremonies

   B. casual parties

   C. sports events

3. _____ entrance ceremonies are held in Japan, this is not usually the case in Britain and the U.S.

   A. Although

   B. Because

   C. However

 NOTES

ceremony: 儀式、式	celebrate: 祝う	traditionally: 伝統的に
graduate: 卒業する	underlined: 下線が引かれた	

 # CHALLENGE YOURSELF! リスニング力を試そう！

Part I PHOTOGRAPHS

A〜Cの英文を聞き、写真の描写として最も適切なものを選びましょう。　🎧 05

1.

A　　B　　C

2.

A　　B　　C

Part II QUESTION-RESPONSE

最初に聞こえてくる英文に対する応答として最も適切なものをA〜Cの中から
選びましょう。　🎧 06

3.　A　　B　　C

4.　A　　B　　C

Part III SHORT CONVERSATIONS

会話を聞き、下の英文が会話の内容と合っていればT（True）、間違っていれば
F（False）を○で囲みましょう。　🎧 07

5.　The cafeteria is busy, but the woman finds a seat.　　　T　　F

6.　The man wants to change his major.　　　T　　F

LET'S READ ALOUD & WRITE! 音読筆写で覚えよう！

授業のまとめとして、今日学習した対話文を3回書き写して
しっかり覚えましょう。1度英文を声に出して読んでから書き
写すと頭に残りやすくなります。

今日のまとめ

英語で答えられますか？　　　What's your major?

How do you like your new school?

文法 一般動詞（現在形）

学生食堂でタカシとキャシー先生の話が続きます。会話では、人を誘ったり、別れ際に挨拶したりする際の表現を学びます。また、文法では一般動詞（現在形）に焦点を当てて学習します。

 WARM-UP　　　　　　　　　　　授業前に確認しておこう！

Vocabulary Preview

1～10の語句の意味として適切なものをa～jの中から選びましょう。　　🎵 08

1. belong to	＿＿＿＿	a.	国際的な
2. continue	＿＿＿＿	b.	2回、2度
3. different	＿＿＿＿	c.	交換
4. exchange	＿＿＿＿	d.	休憩室
5. improve	＿＿＿＿	e.	後で
6. international	＿＿＿＿	f.	～を向上させる
7. introduce	＿＿＿＿	g.	異なった
8. later	＿＿＿＿	h.	紹介する
9. lounge	＿＿＿＿	i.	～に所属する
10. twice	＿＿＿＿	j.	続ける

ビートに乗って1～10の語句を発音してみましょう。

Grammar Point　一般動詞（現在形）

I <u>belong</u> to the school brass band.　　　（私は学校のブラスバンドに所属しています）
Martha <u>lives</u> in the school dormitory.　　（マーサは大学寮に住んでいます）

　be動詞以外の動詞を**一般動詞**と呼びますが、主語が3人称・単数・現在形の場合には動詞の語尾にsやesがつきますので注意が必要です。下の表の空欄に適切な動詞の形を書き入れて確認しましょう。

多くの動詞		語尾にsをつける	like → likes	eat → *eats* want →
-s, -sh, -ch, -x,〈子音字＋o〉で終わる動詞		語尾にesをつける	wash → washes go → goes	catch → do →
yで終わる動詞	母音字＋yの場合	語尾にsをつける	play → plays	buy →
	子音字＋yの場合	yをiに変えてesをつける	study → studies	fly →
例外的な動詞		不規則な変化をする	have → has	

a, i, u, e, o のことを**母音字**、それ以外を**子音字**と言います。

一般動詞の文を否定文にするときは、動詞のすぐ前に don't（= do not）をつけます。また疑問文にするには文の始めに do を持ってきます。主語が 3 人称・単数・現在の場合は doesn't や does を使い、動詞は s や es を外してもとの形（＝原形）に戻します。下の例文の日本語訳を完成させながら確認しましょう。

動詞は原形に戻します。

The school cafeteria **doesn't** open until 11 o'clock.

（ _____ ）

"What **do** you have next period?" "English Conversation."

（ _____ ）

　また、現在の状態や一般的な事実を表すのには**現在時制**を用いますが、その主な用法は下の表のようになります。

「今〜している」のように、現在の動作を表す場合現在進行形（Unit 5）を用います。

現在の状態	Jeff likes his new iPhone.
習慣的な動作	I get up at six every morning.
眼前の動作	Here comes the school bus!
一般的な事実・真理	The sun rises in the east.
物語等での描写	She walks into the room and sits down in front of the fire.

 LET'S LISTEN!　　　　　　　　　　　　会話の大意を聞き取ろう！

タカシとキャシー先生の会話を聞いて、質問に対する答えとして最も適切なものをA〜Cの中から1つ選びましょう。　 09

Question 1｜ Does Takashi belong to any club now?

- A. Yes, he belongs to the tennis club.
- B. Yes, he belongs to the international exchange club.
- C. No, he doesn't.

Question 2｜ How often does the international exchange club meet?

- A. Once a week
- B. Twice a week
- C. Three times a week

Question 3｜ What does Cathy tell Takashi?

- A. Where her office is
- B. Where the International Programs Center is
- C. Where the international exchange club meets

LET'S CHECK & READ ALOUD! 音読してみよう！

1. スクリプトを見ながら会話をもう１度聞き、下線部に当てはまる表現を書き入れましょう。（下線部には単語が２つ入ります）

 09

2. 内容を確認して、全文を音読してみましょう。

3. タカシとキャシー先生の役割をパートナーと一緒に演じてみましょう。

Let's Practice the Roleplay!

Cathy's Role   Takashi's Role

Cathy and Takashi continue to talk at the school cafeteria.

Cathy	How do you like your new school?
Takashi	I ①_____. I have some new friends now.
Cathy	Oh, that's good. Are you in any clubs?
Takashi	No, not yet. I was a member of the tennis club in high school, but I want to try ②_____. I want to improve my English.
Cathy	Then, ③_____ joining the international exchange club? You can meet some exchange students there.
Takashi	Sounds great. ④_____ does this club meet?
Cathy	Twice a week, Tuesday and Thursday at 6 p.m. I sometimes join them.
Takashi	That's fine with me. ⑤_____ they meet?
Cathy	In the lounge in the International Programs Center. Why don't you come this Thursday? I can ⑥_____ to them.
Takashi	Oh, thank you very much. I'll be there.
Cathy	Well, I ⑦_____ go now. It was nice talking to you.
Takashi	Nice talking to you, too. See ⑧_____.

🎵 音読のヒント 🎵

the international exchange club の the をつい「ザ」[ðə] と言ってしまうかもしれませんが、母音で始まる単語の前にある the は「ジ」[ði] と発音します。ただし、unit のように、母音字 u で始まっていても実際の発音が母音で始まらない場合は「ザ」と発音します。

例：the unit [ðə júːnit]

 **GRAMMAR**

A. 例にならい、枠の中から適切な単語を選び、必要な場合は適切な形にして次の1〜4の文を完成させましょう。

例　Rachel (speaks) three languages.

close
teach
speak ✓
work
eat
open

1. My father is a teacher. He (　　　　　　) science at high school.

2. Beth is a nurse. She (　　　　　　) at a hospital near here.

3. Banks usually (　　　　　　) at three in the afternoon.

4. Martha never (　　　　　　) breakfast.

B. 例にならい、カッコ内の指示に従って1〜4の英文を否定文か疑問文に書き換えましょう。

例　Takashi likes his new school. （否定文に）
Takashi doesn't like his new school.

1. We belong to the tennis club. （否定文に）

2. Jenny studies very hard. （否定文に）

3. They come to school by bus. （疑問文に）

4. The cafeteria closes at six p.m. （疑問文に）

C. 日本語の意味に合うようにカッコ内の語句を並べ替え、英文を完成させましょう。ただし、文の始めにくる単語も小文字にしてあり、1つ余分な語句が含まれています。

1. 寮に住んでいるのですか？

(live / do / the dormitory / are / in / you)?

2. みんなはどこによく集まるのですか？

(do / hang / people / out / where / does)?

3. 私たちのクラブは週に2回、火曜日と木曜日に集まります。

(meet / our / meets / a week / twice / club), Tuesday and Thursday.

4. お兄さんもこの学校の生徒なのですか？

(brother / does / is / at / study / your) this school, too?

 **LET'S READ!** 読解力を高めよう！

次のパッセージを読んで 1 〜 3 の質問に答えましょう。 10

Club Activities

Exchange students in Japan are often surprised how seriously Japanese students take part in club activities. In many countries, club and circle activities aren't such a big part of college life. In fact, many students may not even know the difference between clubs and circles. Clubs are officially recognized by the university, while circles are not. Also, clubs often receive <u>financial support</u> from the university, while circles don't. They meet for the purpose of socializing. Outside Japan, students usually prefer to socialize through friendships made in class, or with the friends that they live near.

1. Students in other countries are often _____ active in clubs than Japanese students.

   A. more

   B. less

   C. as

2. Which statement is correct?

   A. Circles are officially recognized by the university.

   B. Circles often receive financial support from the university.

   C. Joining a circle provides opportunities to meet people and make friends.

3. The underlined phrase "financial support" means getting _____ from the university.

   A. career guidance

   B. a health check

   C. money

 **NOTES**

take part in: 〜に参加する   recognize: 認める

socialize: 社交的に活動する   statement: 文

16

 CHALLENGE YOURSELF! リスニング力を試そう！

Part I PHOTOGRAPHS

A～Cの英文を聞き、写真の描写として最も適切なものを選びましょう。 🔊 11

1.

A   B   C

2.

A   B   C

Part II QUESTION-RESPONSE

最初に聞こえてくる英文に対する応答として最も適切なものをA～Cの中から 🔊 12
選びましょう。

3. A   B   C

4. A   B   C

Part III SHORT CONVERSATIONS

会話を聞き、下の英文が会話の内容と合っていればT（True）、間違っていれば 🔊 13
F（False）を○で囲みましょう。

5. The woman is asking where the club practices.   T   F

6. The woman wants to make some foreign friends.   T   F

LET'S READ ALOUD & WRITE! 音読筆写で覚えよう！

授業のまとめとして、今日学習した対話文を3回書き写して
しっかり覚えましょう。1度英文を声に出して読んでから書き
写すと頭に残りやすくなります。

今日のまとめ

英語で答えられますか？   How do you like your school?

UNIT 03 Let me introduce a new member to you.

一般動詞（過去形）

キャシー先生はタカシに留学生のマーサを紹介します。会話では、人を紹介したり、驚きを示したりする際の表現を学びます。また、文法では**一般動詞（過去形）**に焦点を当てて学習します。

 WARM-UP　　　　授業前に確認しておこう！

Vocabulary Preview

1 〜 10 の語句の意味として適切なものを a 〜 j の中から選びましょう。　🔊 14

1. between	＿＿＿	a. 〜を専攻する
2. economics	＿＿＿	b. 〈2つ〉の間に［の、で］
3. have no idea	＿＿＿	c. 心配する
4. major in	＿＿＿	d. 州
5. sophomore	＿＿＿	e. 観光事業
6. state	＿＿＿	f. 経済学
7. still	＿＿＿	g. まだ、いまだに
8. tourism	＿＿＿	h. 〜する間
9. while	＿＿＿	i. まったくわからない
10. worry	＿＿＿	j. 2 年生

ビートに乗って 1 〜 10 の語句を発音してみましょう。

Grammar Point 一般動詞（過去形）

I <u>studied</u> in the library after school yesterday.　（私は昨日の放課後図書館で勉強しました）
Jeff <u>grew</u> up in London.　　　　　　　　　　　　（ジェフはロンドンで育ちました）

　一般動詞の文を過去形にする場合には動詞の最後に ed をつけます。ただし、不規則に変化するものも多いので注意が必要です。巻末資料を参考にしながら下の表の空欄に適切な動詞の過去形を書き入れ確認しましょう。

ほとんどの動詞		語尾に ed をつける	listen → listened	help → helped
-e で終わる動詞		語尾に d をつける	like → liked	use →
y で終わる動詞	母音＋y の場合	語尾に ed をつける	play → played	enjoy →
	子音＋y の場合	y を i に変えて ed をつける	carry → carried	study →
母音1つ＋子音1つで終わる動詞		語尾の子音を重ねて ed をつける	stop → stopped	plan →
例外的な動詞		不規則な変化をする	have → had write → wrote	leave → give →

一般動詞を使った過去形の文を否定文にするときは、動詞のすぐ前に didn't (=did not) をつけます。また疑問文にするには文の始めに did を持ってきます。いずれの場合も動詞は原形に戻します。下の例文の日本語訳を完成させながら確認しましょう。

My bus <u>didn't</u> arrive on time, so I was late for class.

(　_____)

Which high school <u>did</u> you graduate from?

(　_____)

"<u>Did</u> you finish your homework?" "No, I <u>didn't</u> have enough time yesterday."

(　_____)

　また、過去形では「3日前」や「先週の金曜日」のように過去の時を示す表現がよく用いられます。下の表で確認しましょう。

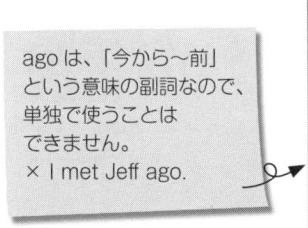

ago は、「今から〜前」という意味の副詞なので、単独で使うことはできません。
× I met Jeff ago.

yesterday	昨日	
the day before yesterday	おととい	
last ...	この前の〜	last Friday, last week
... ago	〜前	three days ago, two hours ago
in ...	〜月に、〜年に	in April, in 2018

① LET'S LISTEN!　　　　　会話の大意を聞き取ろう！

タカシ、マーサ、キャシー先生の会話を聞いて、質問に対する答えとして最も適切なものを A 〜 C の中から 1 つ選びましょう。　 15

Question 1) Which statement is true of Martha?

A. She teaches at Ohio State University.

B. She's a freshman.

C. She's a sophomore.

Question 2) What was Cathy's major?

A. Economics

B. Tourism

C. Psychology

Question 3) Did Cathy stay in Japan while she was in college?

A. Yes, but only for a few days.

B. Yes, for two months.

C. No, she didn't.

LET'S CHECK & READ ALOUD!

音読してみよう！

1. スクリプトを見ながら会話をもう1度聞き、下線部に当てはまる表現を書き入れましょう。（下線部には単語が2つ入ります）

 15

2. 内容を確認して、全文を音読してみましょう。

3. タカシ、マーサ、キャシー先生の役割を3人のグループで演じてみましょう。

Let's Practice the Roleplay!

Cathy's Role

Takashi's Role

Martha's Role

Cathy introduces Takashi to an exchange student, Martha.

Cathy Hi, Martha. ①＿＿＿＿＿＿＿＿ introduce a new member to you. This is Takashi Kudo. Takashi, this is Martha Brown.

Takashi Nice to meet you, Ms. Brown.

Martha Nice to meet you, too. Please call me Martha.

Takashi OK, Martha, and call me Takashi.

Martha OK, Takashi. ②＿＿＿＿＿＿＿＿ our club.

Cathy Martha is from Ohio State University. She's here in the ③＿＿＿＿＿＿＿＿ between the two universities.

Martha I major in economics, Takashi. How ④＿＿＿＿＿＿＿＿?

Takashi I major in psychology, but I'm a freshman and don't know much ⑤＿＿＿＿＿＿＿＿.

Martha Don't worry. I'm a sophomore, but I still don't know much about my major. Cathy, what did you major in?

Cathy I ⑥＿＿＿＿＿＿＿＿ tourism. I ⑦＿＿＿＿＿＿＿＿ Japan for two months while I was in college.

Takashi I ⑧＿＿＿＿＿＿＿＿ idea.

♪ 聞き取りのヒント ♪

"Nice to meet you." の meet you が「ミーチュ」のように発音されることはよく知られていますが、この meet のように [t] で終わる単語のすぐ後に you のような [j] の音で始まる語が来ると、2つの音が一緒になって [tʃ]「チュ」という別の音に変わってしまいます。また、did のように、[d] で終わる単語のすぐ後に [j] の音で始まる語が来た場合も、2つの音が一緒になって [dʒ]「ヂュ」という別の音に変わります。こうした現象を**音の同化**と言います。

 **GRAMMAR**

A. 例にならい、枠の中から適切な単語を選び、必要な場合は適切な形にして次の 1 〜 4 の文を完成させましょう。

例 I (*went*) to bed early last night.

1. We (　　　　　) a good time at the party last night.

2. Cathy (　　　　　) Japanese when she was in college.

3. "What do you (　　　　　) ?" "I'm a student."

4. Let me (　　　　　) myself to you.

> go ✓
> study
> introduce
> do
> play
> have

B. 例にならい、カッコ内の動詞を肯定・否定・疑問のいずれか適切な形に変えて文を完成させましょう。2 は主語として you を補いましょう。

例 We went to the concert, but we _*didn't enjoy*_ it. (enjoy)

1. "Did you talk with Martha this morning?"

   "No, I _____ enough time." (have)

2. "_____ a taxi to the airport?" "No, my father gave me a ride." (take)

3. I went to bed early, but I _____ well last night. (sleep)

4. I _____ a jacket yesterday. I like it very much. (buy)

C. 日本語の意味に合うようにカッコ内の語句を並べ替え、英文を完成させましょう。ただし、文の始めにくる単語も小文字にしてあり、<u>1 つ余分な語句が含まれています</u>。

1. 私は高校の時、吹奏楽部に所属していました。

   (to / belonging / the / brass band / I / belonged) when I was in high school.

   _____

2. 1 年生の時、あの科目を取りましたか？

   (that / take / did / do / course / you) when you were a freshman?

   _____

3. 高校でスポーツは何をしましたか？

   (did / doing / sports / you / which / play) in high school?

   _____

4. 通学にはどのくらい時間がかかりましたか？

   (was / take / did / long / how / it) to come to school?

   _____

次のパッセージを読んで 1～3 の質問に答えましょう。　　 16

School, College or University?

You may hear American students talking about "going back to school."
In the U.S., school is any place where people study and learn. In Britain,
school is not used when talking about university or college. However, in
both countries students may talk about "going to college," and in both
countries this usually means university-level education. People rarely
talk about "going to university" in the U.S. After high school, you "go
to college," even if the college you're attending calls itself a university.
Basically, a college is usually an independent university or part of a
university. For example, Oxford University has over 30 colleges.

1. The meaning of the word "school" in the U.S. is _____ that in the U.K.

   A. the same as

   B. a little different from

   C. completely different from

2. In this passage, Oxford University is used as an example to show that _____.

   A. a college could be part of a university

   B. a college is an independent university

   C. colleges no longer exist in Britain

3. Which statement is correct?

   A. People in the U.S. often talk about "going to university."

   B. Only people in Britain talk about "going to college."

   C. People in both the U.S. and Britain talk about "going to college."

 NOTES

attend: ～に通う　　　　basically: 基本的に　　　　independent: 独立した
Oxford University: オックスフォード大学（イギリスの名門大学）

 CHALLENGE YOURSELF! リスニング力を試そう！

Part I PHOTOGRAPHS

A～Cの英文を聞き、写真の描写として最も適切なものを選びましょう。 17

1.

A　　B　　C

2.

A　　B　　C

Part II QUESTION-RESPONSE

最初に聞こえてくる英文に対する応答として最も適切なものをA～Cの中から選びましょう。 18

3.　A　　B　　C

4.　A　　B　　C

Part III SHORT CONVERSATIONS

会話を聞き、下の英文が会話の内容と合っていればT（True）、間違っていればF（False）を○で囲みましょう。 19

5. The woman is visiting Japan for the first time.　　　　T　　F

6. The man is worried about studying literature.　　　　T　　F

LET'S READ ALOUD & WRITE! 音読筆写で覚えよう！

授業のまとめとして、今日学習した対話文を3回書き写してしっかり覚えましょう。1度英文を声に出して読んでから書き写すと頭に残りやすくなります。

今日のまとめ

英語で答えられますか？　　　Are you in any clubs?

23

UNIT 04 How was your Golden Week?

文法 **未来形**

ゴールデンウィーク明けのある日、タカシとマーサは学生ラウンジで話をします。会話では、予定を述べたり、説明したりする際の表現を学びます。また、文法では**未来形**に焦点を当てて学習します。

 WARM-UP　　　　　　　　　授業前に確認しておこう！

Vocabulary Preview

1 ～ 10 の語句の意味として適切なものを a ～ j の中から選びましょう。　🎵 20

1. by the way	_____	a. 人気がある
2. national holiday	_____	b. 観光地
3. normally	_____	c. 通常は
4. popular	_____	d. くつろぐ、のんびりする
5. bet	_____	e. ところで
6. several	_____	f. ～だと確信している
7. sightseeing spot	_____	g. 疲れた
8. take it easy	_____	h. 寺
9. temple	_____	i. 祝日
10. tired	_____	j. 数個［数人］の

ビートに乗って 1 ～ 10 の語句を発音してみましょう。

Grammar Point 未来形

I'll send you an e-mail later.　　　　　　（後でメールします）
Everything's going to work out.　　　　　（万事うまくいきますよ）

　これから先のことを話す場合には、≪ will + 動詞の原形≫や≪ be going to + 動詞の原形≫といった形を使います。下の表で確認しましょう。

will	意志（～するつもりだ）	I'll be back before lunch.
	予測（～だろう）	Hurry up, or we'll be late for class.
be going to	予測（～だろう）	Hurry! We're going to miss the train.
	計画や意志（～するつもりだ）	We're going to visit Australia in August.

「〜しないだろう」という否定文にするときは、≪ will not ＋ 動詞の原形 ≫や≪ be not going to ＋ 動詞の原形 ≫のように、will や be 動詞のすぐ後に not をつけます。また、「〜するつもりですか？」という疑問文にするには will や be 動詞を主語の前に持ってきます。下の例文の日本語訳を完成させながら確認しましょう。

I'm very sorry. I **won't** be late for class again.

(＿＿＿＿＿＿＿＿＿＿＿＿＿＿＿＿＿＿＿)

> 否定文にするには will の後に not をつけます。will not = won't

If it rains tomorrow, what **will** you do?

(＿＿＿＿＿＿＿＿＿＿＿＿＿＿＿＿＿＿＿)

> 疑問文にするには will を主語の前に持ってきます。

What **are** you **going to** do this weekend?

> 疑問文にするには be 動詞を主語の前に持ってきます。

(＿＿＿＿＿＿＿＿＿＿＿＿＿＿＿＿＿＿＿)

　will と be going to は共に未来を表す表現として使われますが、全く同じ意味というわけではありません。**will は話をしているその場でそうすることに決めたのを表すのに対し、be going to はすでに以前からそのつもりでいたことを表します。**次の例文でその違いを確認しておきましょう。

"I need to clean this room by five." "OK. I'll help you."
（「5 時までにこの部屋を掃除しないといけないんだ」「わかった。手伝うよ」）
"How about going shopping after school?" "Sorry. I'm going to meet a friend of mine."
（「放課後買い物に行くのはどうですか？」「ごめんなさい。友達に会う予定です」）

 ## LET'S LISTEN!

会話の大意を聞き取ろう！

タカシとマーサの会話を聞いて、質問に対する答えとして最も適切なものを A 〜 C の中から 1 つ選びましょう。 21

Question 1) What does Martha ask Takashi?

A. When Golden Week started
B. What Golden Week is
C. What people do during Golden Week

Question 2) Who did Martha go to Kyoto with?

A. With Takashi
B. With her family
C. With her friend

Question 3) What did Takashi do during Golden Week?

A. He visited Tokyo Disneyland.
B. He stayed at home.
C. He went out with Martha.

LET'S CHECK & READ ALOUD!

音読してみよう！

1. スクリプトを見ながら会話をもう1度聞き、下線部に当てはまる表現を書き入れましょう。（下線部には単語が2つ入ります） 21

2. 内容を確認して、全文を音読してみましょう。

3. タカシとマーサの役割をパートナーと一緒に演じてみましょう。

Let's Practice the Roleplay!

Takashi's Role   Martha's Role

Takashi and Martha talk at the student lounge.

| Takashi | How was your Golden Week? |

| Martha | Golden Week? What's that? |

| Takashi | Oh, it's a holiday week in Japan. It ① _____ on April 29th and ends on May 5th. We call this holiday "Golden Week" because it has ② _____ holidays in a week. |

| Martha | I see. Well, I visited Kyoto with my friend last weekend. |

| Takashi | Oh, really? I'm from Kyoto. Where did you go? |

| Martha | We ③ _____ Ginkakuji temple and Kiyomizudera temple. It was a ④ _____ fun. |

| Takashi | They are popular ⑤ _____. I bet they were very crowded. |

| Martha | Yes, they were. We were really tired after the trip. By the way, how ⑥ _____? |

| Takashi | Well, nothing much. I just ⑦ _____ easy at home. But I'm going to visit Tokyo Disneyland this weekend. ⑧ _____ a lot of fun. |

♪ 聞き取りのヒント ♪

went to は「ウェント・トゥー」ではなく「ウェントゥ」のように聞こえます。このように同じ子音が連続する場合、同じ音が繰り返されるのではなく、前の子音が発音されず、その音が聞こえなくなります。例えば、this seat という語のつながりでは [s] の音が連続していますが、この音が2回聞こえるのではなく、[s] の音が1度やや長めに発音されるだけなのです。

A. 例にならい、カッコ内から正しい語句を選び○で囲みましょう。

例 Look at the sky. It (will / (is going to)) rain.

1. "How about going shopping?" "Sorry. (I'll / I'm going to) meet a friend of mine."

2. I'm sorry I was late, Ms. Baker. It (won't / will) happen again.

3. I'm tired. I think (I'll / I) go to bed early.

4. "Is Cathy coming to the party?" "Wait. (I'll / I'm going to) ask her."

B. 例にならい、カッコ内の指示に従って 1 〜 4 の英文を否定文か疑問文に書き換えましょう。

例 I'll call her tonight.（否定文に）　　　　I won't call her tonight.

1. This homework will be finished by tomorrow.（否定文に）

2. My brother is going to major in law.（否定文に）

3. Ms. Baker is going to have a baby next month.（疑問文に）

4. Yuki will join our club, too.（疑問文に）

C. 日本語の意味に合うようにカッコ内の語句を並べ替え、英文を完成させましょう。ただし、文の始めにくる単語も小文字にしてあり、1 つ余分な語句が含まれています。

1. 明日は何をする予定ですか？

(are / will / what / to do / you / going) tomorrow?

2. 後で連絡します。

(back / I'm / I'll / to / you / get) later.

3. 夏休みに京都に戻るつもりですか？

(you / for / will / are / to Kyoto / go back) summer vacation?

4. それは 1 時間で準備できます。

(will / for / in / be / it / ready) an hour.

 **LET'S READ!** 読解力を高めよう！

次のパッセージを読んで 1 〜 3 の質問に答えましょう。 22

Public Holidays

Golden Week is a rare chance for Japanese workers to relax for a few days. Many countries don't need a series of public holidays like Golden Week, because employees have more paid holidays. They can also enjoy longer family vacations. But every country has its own favorite public holidays. In North America, Thanksgiving Day is a good example. The most popular public holidays in Britain are Christmas Day and the day that follows it, Boxing Day. Boxing Day isn't named after the sport! It was the traditional day when churches opened charity boxes and gave money to the poor.

1. Employees in Japan have _____ paid holidays than in many other countries.

   A. as many

   B. fewer

   C. more

2. Traditionally, in Britain, charity boxes were opened and money was given to the poor on _____.

   A. Christmas Day

   B. Boxing Day

   C. Thanksgiving Day

3. Boxing Day comes _____ Christmas Day.

   A. after

   B. before

   C. on

 **NOTES**

paid holiday: 有給休暇   Thanksgiving Day: 感謝祭

Boxing Day: ボクシングデー

CHALLENGE YOURSELF!

リスニング力を試そう！

Part I PHOTOGRAPHS

A ～ C の英文を聞き、写真の描写として最も適切なものを選びましょう。

 23

1.

A   B   C

2.

A   B   C

Part II QUESTION-RESPONSE

最初に聞こえてくる英文に対する応答として最も適切なものを A ～ C の中から
選びましょう。

 24

3. A   B   C

4. A   B   C

Part III SHORT CONVERSATIONS

会話を聞き、下の英文が会話の内容と合っていれば T（True）、間違っていれば
F（False）を○で囲みましょう。

 25

5. The man cleaned his house on the weekend.   T   F

6. The woman visited the fish market in Tokyo.   T   F

LET'S READ ALOUD & WRITE!

音読筆写で覚えよう！

授業のまとめとして、今日学習した対話文を 3 回書き写して
しっかり覚えましょう。1 度英文を声に出して読んでから書き
写すと頭に残りやすくなります。

 今日のまとめ

英語で答えられますか？   How was your weekend?

29

UNIT 05 I'm looking for a part-time job.

学生ラウンジでタカシとマーサの話が続きます。
会話では、詳細を尋ねたり、理由を述べたりする
際の表現を学びます。また、文法では進行形に焦
点を当てて学習します。

 WARM-UP

授業前に確認しておこう！

Vocabulary Preview

1 〜 10 の語句の意味として適切なものを a 〜 j の中から選びましょう。　🎧 26

1. around	＿＿＿	a. 実は	
2. at first	＿＿＿	b. 最初は	
3. get off	＿＿＿	c. 〜のあちこちに	
4. in fact	＿＿＿	d. 〜を探す	
5. look for	＿＿＿	e. アルバイト	
6. friendly	＿＿＿	f. 〜に慣れて	
7. part-time job	＿＿＿	g. 普段は	
8. shift	＿＿＿	h. 交代勤務時間	
9. used to	＿＿＿	i. 優しい、親切な	
10. usually	＿＿＿	j.（仕事から）解放される、終える	

ビートに乗って 1 〜 10 の語句を発音してみましょう。

Grammar Point　進行形

I <u>work</u> part-time at a bookstore.　　（私は書店でアルバイトをしています）〔現在形〕
I'm <u>working</u> right now.　　（私は今仕事中です）〔現在進行形〕
I <u>was working</u> at that time.　　（私はそのとき仕事をしていました）〔過去進行形〕

　一般に現在形は日常的な内容を指すのに対し、今している最中の動作を表す場合には現在進行形を用い、《 be 動詞 + 動詞の ing 形》の形で表します。下の表の空欄に適切な動詞の形を書き入れて動詞の ing 形の作り方を確認しましょう。

ほとんどの動詞	語尾に ing をつける	work → working	eat → *eating*
子音＋e で終わる動詞	語尾の e を取って ing をつける	make → making	give →
-ie [ai] で終わる動詞	語尾の ie を y に変えて ing をつける	lie → lying	die →
1 母音＋1 子音で終わる動詞	語尾の子音字を重ねて ing をつける	get → getting	begin →

現在進行形は、「〜している」のように今実際にしていることだけではなく、**すでに決まっている予定**を表すこともあります。また、過去形の be 動詞を使って**過去進行形**にすると「〜していた」という意味を表します。下の例文の日本語訳を完成させながら使い方を確認しましょう。

My parents <u>are coming</u> from Kyoto this weekend.

(_____)

否定文にするときは、be 動詞のすぐ後に not をつけます。

<u>I'm not</u> joking. <u>I'm telling</u> the truth.

(_____)

疑問文にするには be 動詞を主語の前に持ってきます。

We called you many times. What <u>were</u> you <u>doing</u>?

(_____)

進行形は「〜している」のように動作を表すものですから、know（知っている）などのように状態を表す動詞は通常進行形にはなりません。ただし、have や live のように状態を表す動詞でも、次のような場合は進行形にすることができます。

We<u>'re having</u> lunch now.　　（今昼食を取っている最中です）

※この have は「食べる」という意味

My father has a home in Kyoto, but he<u>'s living</u> in London now on business.

（父は京都に自宅がありますが、今は仕事でロンドンに住んでいます）

※ live は一般に「住んでいる」という状態を表しますが、進行形にすると「ずっとそこに住むわけではなく、一時的に住んでいる」という意味になります。

① LET'S LISTEN!　　　　会話の大意を聞き取ろう！

タカシとマーサの会話を聞いて、質問に対する答えとして最も適切なものを A 〜 C の中から 1 つ選びましょう。　 27

Question 1 When did Takashi start working part-time?

A. Last week

B. Last month

C. Three months ago

Question 2 What does Takashi say about his job?

A. He works only on weekends.

B. His shift usually ends at seven p.m.

C. The manager is kind to him.

Question 3 Does Martha want to work part-time?

A. Yes, she needs to save money for a trip.

B. Yes, she has a lot of time during the summer vacation.

C. No, she needs more time to study Japanese.

LET'S CHECK & READ ALOUD!　　　　音読してみよう！

1. スクリプトを見ながら会話をもう１度聞き、下線部に当てはまる表現を書き入れましょう。（下線部には単語が２つ入ります） 27

2. 内容を確認して、全文を音読してみましょう。

3. タカシとマーサの役割をパートナーと一緒に演じてみましょう。

Let's Practice the Roleplay!

Martha's Role　Takashi's Role

Martha and Takashi continue to talk at the student lounge.

| Martha | I'm ①_____ a part-time job. Do you have one, Takashi? |

| Takashi | Oh, yes. In fact, I just started ②_____ a restaurant near here last month. |

| Martha | Do you work on weekends? |

| Takashi | No, I work three nights a week after class. ③_____ usually starts at seven p.m. and I ④_____ at 11. |

| Martha | Is it hard? |

| Takashi | Well, at first it was difficult, but I soon ⑤_____ to it. The manager is kind and all the ⑥_____ are really friendly. |

| Martha | Do you think I could do the job, too? |

| Takashi | Of course, you can. But why do you need the job? |

| Martha | I want to ⑦_____ Japan during the summer vacation, so I need to save enough money by then. ⑧_____ good for my Japanese, too. |

♪♫ 聞き取りのヒント ♫♪

クッキングやウォーキングなど、カタカナ英語の影響もあって、working など動詞の ing 形を「ワーキング」のように「〜イング」と発音する人がいますが、ing の [iŋ] における [ŋ] は「ング」という感じの鼻にかけた音で、「グ」の音は鼻から出ていくため、はっきりとは聞こえない音です。「イング」ではなく、「イング」という感じです。発音する際にも気をつけたいものです。

A. 例にならい、枠の中から適切な単語を選び、必要な場合は適切な形にして次の1～4の文を完成させましょう。

例　Turn off the television. We (*are studying*) now.

1. I (　　　　　　　　　) right now. Can I call you later?

2. It (　　　　　　　　　) now. Take an umbrella.

3. I'm so tired. I (　　　　　　　　　) to go to bed now.

4. "Where is Jenny?" "She (　　　　　　　　　) a shower."

> study ✓
> want
> take
> work
> rain

B. 例にならい、次の英文をカッコ内の指示に従って書き換えましょう。

例　Jeff reads the letter. (now を加えて現在進行形に)

Jeff is reading the letter now.

1. Martha doesn't cook. (now を加えて現在進行形に)

_____

2. What did you do? (at that time を加えて過去進行形に)

_____

3. Does William use this computer? (now を加えて現在進行形に)

_____

4. We have lunch with Cathy. (at that time を加えて過去進行形に)

_____

C. 日本語の意味に合うようにカッコ内の語句を並べ替え、英文を完成させましょう。ただし、文の始めにくる単語も小文字にしてあり、1つ余分な語句が含まれています。

1. 何かを買うためにお金を貯めていますか？

(saving / to / do / you / money / are) buy something?

_____

2. マーサはアルバイトを探しているところです。

(looking / at / Martha / for / a part-time job / is) .

_____

3. 私たちは野球部に所属しています。

(the / baseball club / we / belong / are belonging / to) .

_____

4. 授業の予習をしているのかい？

(preparing / your class / are / do / for / you) ?

_____

 **LET'S READ!** 読解力を高めよう！

次のパッセージを読んで１〜３の質問に答えましょう。 28

How Were Your SAT Scores?

You may hear American high school students talking about SAT scores. The SAT is a test for college <u>admissions</u> in the United States. It is held seven times a year, and is an important part of the college admission process. The test is in three parts: Critical Reading, Mathematics, and Writing, with a maximum score of 2,400 points. Some colleges make SAT scores an optional part of their admission process. They say that a student's high school Grade Point Average (GPA) is a better indicator of ability. But for most students, <u>the SAT remains an important hurdle</u> to clear before finding a place in higher education.

1. The underlined word "admissions" is closest in meaning to _____.

   A. graduates

   B. acceptance

   C. dormitories

2. Which statement is correct?

   A. All colleges require high school students to submit an SAT score and a GPA score.

   B. Some colleges do not use SAT scores in their admission process.

   C. Students in the U.S. can choose to send colleges their high school GPA instead of taking the SAT.

3. The underlined part "the SAT remains an important hurdle" means "the SAT _____ an important part."

   A. is never

   B. is still

   C. used to be

> **NOTES**
>
> Critical Reading: クリティカル・リーディング
> （文章のポイントを的確に見抜き、「批判する力」を育むための文章読解法）
>
> optional: 選択式の
>
> GPA: 学業平均値
> （各科目の成績から特定の方式によって算出された学生の成績評価値で、学力を測る指標となる）
>
> indicator: 指し示すもの
>
> closest in meaning to: 〜に意味が最も近い

CHALLENGE YOURSELF!

Part I　PHOTOGRAPHS

A ～ C の英文を聞き、写真の描写として最も適切なものを選びましょう。　🎧 29

1.　　A　　B　　C

2.　　A　　B　　C

Part II　QUESTION-RESPONSE

最初に聞こえてくる英文に対する応答として最も適切なものを A ～ C の中から
選びましょう。　🎧 30

3.　A　　B　　C

4.　A　　B　　C

Part III　SHORT CONVERSATIONS

会話を聞き、下の英文が会話の内容と合っていれば T（True）、間違っていれば
F（False）を○で囲みましょう。　🎧 31

5. The man works at night.　　　　　　　　　　　　　　　T　　　F

6. The man told the woman to change her apartment.　　　T　　　F

LET'S READ ALOUD & WRITE!

授業のまとめとして、今日学習した対話文を 3 回書き写して
しっかり覚えましょう。1 度英文を声に出して読んでから書き
写すと頭に残りやすくなります。

今日のまとめ

英語で答えられますか？　　　Do you have a part-time job?

UNIT 06 What do you call this in Japanese?

タカシとマーサは学生食堂で昼食について話をしています。会話では、意向を尋ねたり、好みを述べたりする際の表現を学びます。また、文法では**受動態**に焦点を当てて学習します。

WARM-UP

授業前に確認しておこう！

Vocabulary Preview

1 ～ 10 の語句の意味として適切なものを a ～ j の中から選びましょう。　　　　🎵 CD 32

1. bowl	_____		a.	～を意味する
2. care for	_____		b.	とてもおいしい
3. delicious	_____		c.	料理
4. dish	_____		d.	むしろ～の方を好む
5. favorite	_____		e.	椀、丼
6. mean	_____		f.	トンカツ
7. perfect	_____		g.	申し分ない、理想的な
8. pork cutlet	_____		h.	～を好む
9. prefer	_____		i.	様々な
10. various	_____		j.	お気に入り

ビートに乗って 1 ～ 10 の語句を発音してみましょう。

Grammar Point　受動態

Martha **made** our club's website.

（マーサがクラブのホームページを作りました）〔能動態〕

Our club's website **was made** by Martha.

（クラブのホームページはマーサによって作られました）〔受動態〕

「～によって」は by で表しますが、誰がしたのかが重要でない場合には不要です。

「～は…される／されている」のように、何らかの動作を受ける意味を表す場合には、**受動態**を用い、≪ be 動詞 + 過去分詞≫という形で表します。これに対して、これまで学習してきた「～は…する」のように、何かに働きかける意味を表す文を**能動態**と言います。

能動態にするか受動態にするかは、話題になっている「もの」や「こと」によって決まります。次の例文では、話題が「インスタグラム」なので受動態が使われるわけです。

Instagram is very popular now. It **is used** around the world.

（インスタグラムは現在とても人気があります。それは世界中で使われています）

この例文は "People use it around the world." のように能動態で表現することも可能ですが、受動態で表現する方が自然です。

また、過去分詞は、talk → talked（過去形）→ talked（過去分詞）のように、多くの場合動詞の過去形と同じ形ですが、eat → ate（過去形）→ eaten（過去分詞）のように不規則に変化するものもあります。巻末資料を参考にしながら下の表の空欄に適切な動詞の形を書き入れ確認しましょう。

不規則動詞の変化パターン		原形	過去形	過去分詞形
A-A-A	原形、過去形、過去分詞がすべて同じ	cut cost	cut	cut
A-B-A	原形と過去分詞が同じ	come run		
A-B-B	過去形と過去分詞が同じ	tell think		
A-B-C	原形、過去形、過去分詞がすべて異なる	go know		

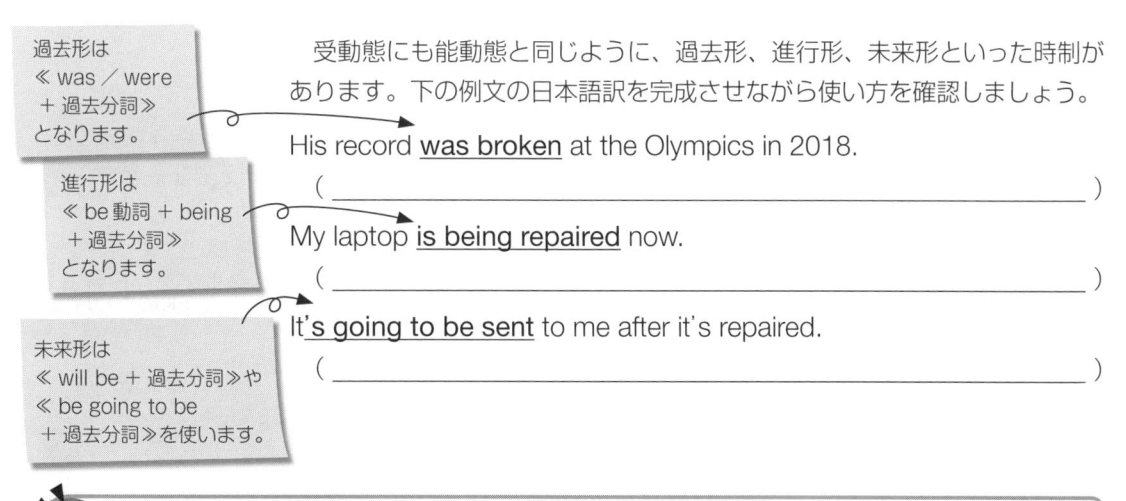

過去形は
≪ was ／ were
＋過去分詞≫
となります。

受動態にも能動態と同じように、過去形、進行形、未来形といった時制があります。下の例文の日本語訳を完成させながら使い方を確認しましょう。

His record <u>was broken</u> at the Olympics in 2018.

(_____)

進行形は
≪ be 動詞 + being
＋過去分詞≫
となります。

My laptop <u>is being repaired</u> now.

(_____)

未来形は
≪ will be ＋過去分詞≫や
≪ be going to be
＋過去分詞≫を使います。

It<u>'s going to be sent</u> to me after it's repaired.

(_____)

🎵 ① LET'S LISTEN!

会話の大意を聞き取ろう！

タカシとマーサの会話を聞いて、質問に対する答えとして最も適切なものを A 〜 C の中から 1 つ選びましょう。 33

Question 1 ⟩ What is Takashi going to order?

A. Gyudon

B. Katsudon

C. Oyakodon

Question 2 ⟩ What kind of meat does Martha like?

A. Pork

B. Chicken

C. Beef

Question 3 ⟩ What does Takashi say about rice bowl dishes?

A. The cafeteria is popular for delicious rice bowl dishes.

B. He doesn't care for them very much.

C. There are many kinds of rice bowl dishes.

LET'S CHECK & READ ALOUD!

音読してみよう！

1. スクリプトを見ながら会話をもう１度聞き、下線部に当てはまる表現を書き入れましょう。（下線部には単語が２つ入ります） 33

2. 内容を確認して、全文を音読してみましょう。

3. タカシとマーサの役割をパートナーと一緒に演じてみましょう。

Let's Practice the Roleplay!

Martha's Role   Takashi's Role

Martha and Takashi look at the menu stand in the school cafeteria.

Martha	What are you going to have today, Takashi?
Takashi	Well, I think ①_____ this pork cutlet rice bowl.
Martha	I'm still not ②_____ reading kanji. What do you call it in Japanese?
Takashi	It's called *katsudon*. It's one of ③_____. Would you like to try it?
Martha	Well, it ④_____, but I don't ⑤_____ pork very much. I prefer chicken.
Takashi	I see. Then, how about this one? It's a chicken and egg rice bowl.
Martha	Sounds perfect.
Takashi	⑥_____ *oyakodon*.
Martha	So *don* ⑦_____ a rice bowl dish, right?
Takashi	Yes, that's right. There are ⑧_____ of rice bowl dishes.

♪ 聞き取りのヒント ♪

単語の最後にくる l [l] は、つづり字からつい「ル」に近い音を予想しますが、実際には「ゥ」のように聞こえます。例えば、well [wél] は「ウェル」ではなく、むしろ「ウェゥ」のように聞こえます。bowl [bóul] も「ボウル」ではなく「ボウゥ」のような感じです。I'll もつい「アイル」と発音しがちですが、「アィゥ」が実際の発音に近いものです。

 **GRAMMAR**

A. 例にならい、枠の中から適切な単語を選び、必要な場合は適切な形にして次の1～4の文を完成させましょう。

例 Soccer (*is played*) in many countries.

1. The meeting will (   ) here.
2. This temple (   ) about 500 years ago.
3. The new school song will (   ) by a famous artist.
4. This area (   ) by the typhoon last week.

| hit |
| hold |
| play ✓ |
| build |
| write |

B. 例にならい、カッコ内から正しい語句を選び○で囲みましょう。

例 This table (makes / (is made)) of wood.

1. The song can (download / be downloaded) off the Internet.
2. My laptop (fell / was fallen) off the desk and broke.
3. The test will (cover / be covered) the first four units of the textbook.
4. This town is known (by / for) its old temples.

C. 日本語の意味に合うようにカッコ内の語句を並べ替え、英文を完成させましょう。ただし、文の始めにくる単語も小文字にしてあり、<u>1つ余分な語句が含まれています</u>。

1. 大雨のためすべての授業が休講になりました。

(canceling / canceled / to / due / were / all the classes) heavy rain.

_____

2. その結果は明日連絡される予定です。

(the / result / given / giving / will / be) tomorrow.

_____

3. その教科書はすぐに返却されなければなりません。

(the / returned / return / be / must / textbook) soon.

_____

4. 私のパソコンは現在修理中です。

(computer / being / been / my / repaired / is) at the moment.

_____

次のパッセージを読んで 1 〜 3 の質問に答えましょう。   34

The Gap Year

In the U.K. and Australia, many students don't enter a university soon after they have been accepted. Instead, they delay their entrance, usually for a year, taking a "gap year." This break from education allows them to experience a year in the real world. It also gives them opportunities to look back and consider why they are going to university. Gap year students often work to save money for university, travel, or do volunteer work. After taking a one-year break, students are usually more focused on studying. Gap years are less common in the U.S., but are rapidly gaining popularity.

1. A gap year gives students the opportunity to _____.

   A. experience life outside school

   B. get good high school grades

   C. take university entrance examinations once again

2. Students on gap years often choose to _____.

   A. apply to a different university

   B. help other people

   C. take extra classes in high school

3. Gap years _____.

   A. are more popular in the U.S. than in the U.K.

   B. started in the U.S., not in the U.K.

   C. are also becoming popular in the U.S.

 NOTES

gap year: ギャップ・イヤー（高等学校卒業から大学入学までの期間）

accept: 受け入れる   delay: 〜を遅らせる

 **CHALLENGE YOURSELF!**

Part I PHOTOGRAPHS

A 〜 C の英文を聞き、写真の描写として最も適切なものを選びましょう。 35

1.

A　　B　　C

2.

A　　B　　C

Part II QUESTION-RESPONSE

最初に聞こえてくる英文に対する応答として最も適切なものを A 〜 C の中から
選びましょう。 35 36

3. A　　B　　C

4. A　　B　　C

Part III SHORT CONVERSATIONS

会話を聞き、下の英文が会話の内容と合っていれば T（True）、間違っていれば 37
F（False）を○で囲みましょう。

5. The woman is telling the man about a rice dish.　　　　　　　　　T　　　　F

6. The man can't eat sushi or sashimi.　　　　　　　　　　　　　　　T　　　　F

LET'S READ ALOUD & WRITE!

授業のまとめとして、今日学習した対話文を 3 回書き写して
しっかり覚えましょう。1 度英文を声に出して読んでから書き
写すと頭に残りやすくなります。

今日のまとめ

英語で答えられますか？　　　What's your favorite rice bowl dish?

Have you been there?

現在完了形

タカシとマーサは部室で話をしています。マーサは何か手伝ってほしいことがあるようです。会話では、経験を尋ねたり、提案したりする際の表現を学びます。また、文法では**現在完了形**に焦点を当てて学習します。

WARM-UP

授業前に確認しておこう！

Vocabulary Preview

1 ～ 10 の語句の意味として適切なものを a ～ j の中から選びましょう。　　 38

1. budget	_____	a.	招待客
2. excellent	_____	b.	予算
3. contact	_____	c.	極めて良い
4. farewell	_____	d.	出発する
5. leave	_____	e.	（値段などが）手ごろな
6. guest	_____	f.	かなり、非常に
7. prepare	_____	g.	連絡を取る
8. price	_____	h.	価格
9. quite	_____	i.	準備する
10. reasonable	_____	j.	別れの

ビートに乗って 1 ～ 10 の語句を発音してみましょう。

Grammar Point　現在完了形

I'<u>ve</u> already <u>contacted</u> the club members, so they will be here soon.

（部員はすでに連絡したので、すぐにここに来ますよ）

My train <u>hasn't arrived</u> yet, so I'll be a little late.

（私の乗る電車がまだ到着していませんので少し遅れます）

<u>Have</u> you <u>finished</u> your homework yet?

（宿題はもう済ませましたか？）

否定文にするにはhave/has の後にnot をつけます。

疑問文にするにはhave/has を主語の前に持ってきます。

過去にしたことや過去に起こったことを現在と結びつけて話す場合には**現在完了形**を用い、≪ have/has ＋ 過去分詞≫という形で表します。主語が he など 3 人称単数の場合は have ではなく has を使います。

　また、現在完了形の表す意味にはいくつか種類があります。次の表の例文の日本語訳を完成させながらそれぞれの意味を確認しましょう。

完了	～したところだ	"How about lunch together?" "Sorry. We've just eaten." (　　　　　　　　　　　　　　　　　　　　　　)
	～してしまった	I've lost my wallet. What should I do? (　　　　　　　　　　　　　　　　　　　　　　)
経験	～したことがある	"Have you ever been to Kyoto?" "Yes, but only once." (　　　　　　　　　　　　　　　　　　　　　　)
継続	ずっと～している	Cathy has been a teacher for 20 years. (　　　　　　　　　　　　　　　　　　　　　　)

　現在完了形は、あくまで現在の状況を述べる言い方なので、yesterday など、明確に過去の時点を表す表現とは一緒に使うことができません。

 ## LET'S LISTEN!

会話の大意を聞き取ろう！

タカシとマーサの会話を聞いて、質問に対する答えとして最も適切なものを A ～ C の中から 1 つ選びましょう。　 39

Question 1) Which sentence is true of Greg?

A. He's coming from England.
B. He's traveling around Japan next month.
C. He's leaving Japan.

Question 2) What does Martha ask Takashi to do?

A. Help her find a place for the party
B. Help her make a list of guests
C. Tell Greg about the party

Question 3) What does Takashi say about the restaurant?

A. It's an excellent French restaurant.
B. The price is not so high.
C. It's a little far from the school.

LET'S CHECK & READ ALOUD!　　　　　　音読してみよう！

1. スクリプトを見ながら会話をもう１度聞き、下線部に当てはまる表現を書き入れましょう。（下線部には単語が２つ入ります） 39

2. 内容を確認して、全文を音読してみましょう。

3. タカシとマーサの役割をパートナーと一緒に演じてみましょう。

Let's Practice the Roleplay!

Takashi's Role　　Martha's Role

Takashi speaks to Martha at the clubroom.

Takashi	Hi, Martha. What's up?
Martha	Nothing much. I'm ①_____ Greg's farewell party.
Takashi	Oh, he's going back to England, right?
Martha	That's right. ②_____ next month. Could you help me?
Takashi	Sure. What ③_____ do?
Martha	Well, ④_____ a list of guests, so I'll start looking for a good place to have the party. Can you help me find it?
Takashi	Of course. How much is ⑤_____?
Martha	About 3,000 yen per person.
Takashi	Well, there's a good Italian restaurant near here. It's called Marco's. Have you ⑥_____?
Martha	No, I haven't.
Takashi	Then, why ⑦_____ go there tonight? The food is excellent, and the price is ⑧_____. Also, it's not far from here.
Martha	Sounds great.

🎵 聞き取りのヒント 🎵

実際の会話では、１語ずつ区切って発音されることはなく、単語と単語がつながって聞こえることがあります。これを**音の連結**と言い、例えば can I は「キャン・アイ」ではなく「キャナイ」のように聞こえます。「連結」は、「子音で終わる単語」の後に「母音で始まる単語」が続いた場合によく起こります。

 **GRAMMAR** 文法に強くなろう！

A. 例にならい、枠の中から適切な単語を選び、必要な場合は適切な形にして次の1〜4の文を完成させましょう。

> 例　The weather （ was ） fine yesterday.

1. "Is Takashi here?" "No, he's just （　　　　　） ."
2. I've already （　　　　　） my homework.
3. "Why don't we have lunch?" "Sorry. We've just （　　　　　） ."
4. Oh, no! I've （　　　　　） the exam again.

> do
> leave
> fail
> eat
> be ✓

B. 例にならい、カッコ内から正しい語句を選び○で囲みましょう。

> 例　（ Have you seen / (Did you see)) Cathy yesterday?

1. We （ held / have held ） a farewell party for Greg last night.
2. Jenny and I are good friends. （ I know / I've known ） her for three years.
3. Martha has been in Kyoto （ since / for ） yesterday.
4. I （ read / have read ） *Harry Potter* when I was a child.

C. 日本語の意味に合うようにカッコ内の語句を並べ替え、英文を完成させましょう。ただし、文の始めにくる単語も小文字にしてあり、1つ余分な語句が含まれています。

1. 私は1度も恋愛したことがありません。

   （ never / love / I've / be / in / been ） .

   _____

2. 知り合ってどれくらいになるのですか？

   （ have / known / knew / long / you / how ） each other?

   _____

3. グレッグはちょうどイングランドに出発したところです。

   （ England / left / leaving / for / Greg / has just ） .

   _____

4. ここで働いて半年になります。

   （ since / for / worked / six / here / I've ） months.

   _____

次のパッセージを読んで 1 ～ 3 の質問に答えましょう。 40

Freshers' Week

One of the biggest cultural differences between Japanese, American and British campus life is that in Britain, every campus will have a bar. This surprises many Japanese students, because they can't <u>legally</u> drink alcohol until they are 20. In the U.S., the age limit is usually 21. But in Britain, students can drink from 18. For many British students, their first introduction to student life is "Freshers' Week." It's a program of events and parties that often involves heavy drinking. Not surprisingly, this can lead to problems for some students, but Freshers' Week parties and the campus bar are an important part of students' social life.

1. The underlined word "legally" means "_____".

   A. against the law

   B. breaking the law

   C. within the law

2. British students start drinking alcohol much _____ than students in Japan or the U.S.

   A. earlier

   B. faster

   C. later

3. "Freshers' Week" has a series of events to _____ new students to university life.

   A. drink

   B. teach

   C. introduce

 NOTES

Freshers' Week: 新入生歓迎週間   bar: バー、酒場

CHALLENGE YOURSELF! リスニング力を試そう！

Part I PHOTOGRAPHS

A～Cの英文を聞き、写真の描写として最も適切なものを選びましょう。 41

1.

　　　A　　B　　C

2.

　　　A　　B　　C

Part II QUESTION-RESPONSE

最初に聞こえてくる英文に対する応答として最も適切なものをA～Cの中から
選びましょう。 42

3.　A　　B　　C

4.　A　　B　　C

Part III SHORT CONVERSATIONS

会話を聞き、下の英文が会話の内容と合っていればT（True）、間違っていれば
F（False）を○で囲みましょう。 43

5. The woman wants the man to go back to England.　　　　T　　F

6. The man doesn't think the restaurant is too expensive.　　T　　F

 **LET'S READ ALOUD & WRITE!** 音読筆写で覚えよう！

授業のまとめとして、今日学習した対話文を3回書き写して
しっかり覚えましょう。1度英文を声に出して読んでから書き
写すと頭に残りやすくなります。

今日のまとめ

英語で答えられますか？　　　Have you been to England?

UNIT 08 Could you tell me how to get there?

文法　助動詞

留学生のジェニーは道に迷ってしまい、路上で通行人に話しかけます。会話では、道順を尋ねたり、感謝したりする際の表現を学びます。また、文法では**助動詞**に焦点を当てて学習します。

 WARM-UP　　　　　　　　　　　　授業前に確認しておこう！

Vocabulary Preview

1 ～ 10 の語句の意味として適切なものを a ～ j の中から選びましょう。　　🎵 44

1. appreciate	_____	a.	感謝する
2. convenience	_____	b.	～を見逃す
3. hurry	_____	c.	～を口にする、～に言及する
4. less	_____	d.	真っすぐに
5. lost	_____	e.	より少なく
6. mention	_____	f.	便利さ
7. miss	_____	g.	～のそばを（通り）過ぎて
8. museum	_____	h.	博物館
9. past	_____	i.	道に迷った
10. straight	_____	j.	急ぐ

ビートに乗って 1 ～ 10 の語句を発音してみましょう。

Grammar Point 助動詞

You **must** be joking.　　　　　　　　　　　（冗談でしょう）

Could you tell me the way to the station?　　（駅への道順を教えていただけませんか？）

助動詞は**動詞の前につけて動詞に意味を追加するもの**です。助動詞の場合、一般動詞と違って主語が 3 人称単数であっても語尾に –s や –es がつくことはありません。

主な助動詞とその用法は下の表の通りです。

can	～できる（be able to） ～してもよい	must	～しなければならない（have to） ～に違いない
may	～してもよい ～かもしれない	might	～かもしれない
should	～すべきである	used to	以前は～だった

must の否定形 must not は「〜してはいけない」という意味になり、「〜する必要はない」と言いたい場合は don't have to を使います。また、would と could はそれぞれ助動詞 will と can の過去形ですが、実際のコミュニケーションにおいては過去の意味で使うのではなく、丁寧な言い方をする場合によく用いられます。

would like	〜をいただきたいのですが	※ want や want to よりも丁寧で控えめな感じがします。
would like to	〜したいのですが	
Would you ... ?	〜していただけないでしょうか？	※ Will you ... ? や Can you ... ? よりも丁寧で控えめな感じがします。
Could you ... ?		

上の表を参考にして、下の例文の日本語訳を完成させましょう。

I feel sick. <u>May</u> I leave the room for a while?

(_____)

> 疑問文にするときは助動詞を文の始めに置きます。

You <u>shouldn't</u> spend so much money on computer games.

(_____)

> 否定文にするときは助動詞のすぐ後に not をつけます。

"What day <u>shall</u> we meet?" "How about this Saturday?"

(_____)

I'<u>d like</u> the receipt, please. (_____)

I'<u>d like to</u> introduce someone. (_____)

<u>Would</u> you help me move this table? (_____)

① LET'S LISTEN!

会話の大意を聞き取ろう！

ジェニーと通行人の男性の会話を聞いて、質問に対する答えとして最も適切なものをＡ〜Ｃの中から１つ選びましょう。

🎵 45

Question 1 Where does Jenny want to go?

A. A convenience store

B. The museum

C. The city hall

Question 2 How long does it take to go there?

A. About five minutes

B. Less than 10 minutes

C. Fifteen minutes

Question 3 What should Jenny do at the corner?

A. She should turn right.

B. She should turn left.

C. She should go straight.

LET'S CHECK & READ ALOUD!　　音読してみよう！

1. スクリプトを見ながら会話をもう１度聞き、下線部に当てはまる表現を書き入れ
   ましょう。（下線部には単語が２つ入ります）　 45
2. 内容を確認して、全文を音読してみましょう。
3. ジェニーと通行人の役割をパートナーと一緒に演じてみましょう。

Let's Practice the Roleplay!

Jenny's Role　　Passerby's Role

Jenny speaks to a man walking on the street.

| Jenny | Excuse me. Could you help me? I think ①_____. |

| Passerby | Sure. Where would you like to go? |

| Jenny | I'd like to go to the city museum. Is it far from here? |

| Passerby | No, it isn't. You ②_____ there in ③_____ 10 minutes. |

| Jenny | Good. Could you tell me how to get there? |

| Passerby | Of course. Go straight and ④_____ the convenience store. Then, turn right at the corner. The museum is ⑤_____ left. |

| Jenny | Turn right at the corner and it's on my left. Is that right? |

| Passerby | Yes, that's right. You ⑥_____ it. |

| Jenny | Oh, thank you. I really ⑦_____ kindness. |

| Passerby | Don't ⑧_____. I'd hurry if I were you. The museum closes at five. |

| Jenny | Oh, right. Thanks again. |

♪ 聞き取りのヒント ♪

can と can't の聞き分けはなかなか難しいものです。can't の語尾 [t] ははっきりと聞こえないこと
が多いですから、[t] の音が聞こえるか聞こえないかよりも、文の中でそこに強勢があるかないかに
着目した方がよいでしょう。否定形 can't [kǽnt] は、<u>強く、はっきりと、長めに</u>発音され、「キャント」
のように聞こえます。反対に、can には通常アクセントがなく、<u>弱く、曖昧に、短く</u>発音され、[kən]「カ
ン」や [kn]「クン」のように聞こえます。ただし、"Yes, I can." と答える場合など、文末に来た場
合や特に強調したい場合は [kǽn]「キャン」と発音されます。

 **GRAMMAR**

文法に強くなろう！

A. 例にならい、枠の中から適切な語句を選んで次の 1 ～ 4 の文を完成させましょう。

> 例　I (*would like*) the receipt, please.

1. Excuse me. (　　　　　　　) I ask you something?
2. Time is money, so we (　　　　　　) waste it.
3. I (　　　　　　) hate English, but now I like it.
4. You don't (　　　　　　) do everything. We'll help you.

shouldn't
used to
would like ✓
may
have to

B. 例にならい、カッコ内から正しい語句を選び○で囲みましょう。

> 例　I don't believe it. It (can /(can't)) be true.

1. (I'd like / I'd like to) a table for five, please.
2. I'm very sorry, Ms. Baker, but I (have to / have) miss class next week.
3. (Could I / Could you) borrow your pen?
4. What club (would you like / would you like to) join?

C. 日本語の意味に合うようにカッコ内の語句を並べ替え、英文を完成させましょう。ただし、文の始めにくる単語も小文字にしてあり、1 つ余分な語句が含まれています。

1. ちょっと教えてもらってもいいですか？

   (you / a / can you / quick / can I / ask) question?

   _____

2. サークルのイベントに何をしましょうか？

   (do / we / what / does / should / for) our club event?

   _____

3. その考えは良いと思いますが、費用がかかり過ぎるかもしれません。

   I like the idea, but (too / might / it / is / expensive / be).

   _____

4. 悪いけど、もう授業に行かないといけないんだ。

   Sorry, (get / to class / must / have / I / to).

   _____

 **LET'S READ!**

次のパッセージを読んで 1 ～ 3 の質問に答えましょう。 46

Dormitory Life

Dormitory life has changed a lot in recent years. In the past, students were happy to cut costs by living in cheap accommodations with shared rooms and shared facilities. However, these days, students expect more comfort, so many universities offer private rooms with private toilet and shower facilities. In Britain, students usually only spend their first year in a dormitory—known as a "hall of residence." After the first year it's cheaper and usually more fun to share a rented apartment with friends. Of course, local students don't usually stay in dormitories at all. Most will save money by continuing to live at home with their parents.

1. In recent years, the quality of student accommodations has _____.

   A. got worse

   B. improved

   C. stayed the same

2. In the U.K., dormitories are usually called _____.

   A. rented apartments

   B. private rooms

   C. halls of residence

3. Most British students use dormitory accommodations only for _____.

   A. the first semester

   B. the first year

   C. the first two years

 **NOTES**

accommodation: 宿泊施設   facility: 設備

comfort: 快適さ

CHALLENGE YOURSELF!

リスニング力を試そう！

Part I PHOTOGRAPHS

A ～ C の英文を聞き、写真の描写として最も適切なものを選びましょう。 47

1.

A   B   C

2.

A   B   C

Part II QUESTION-RESPONSE

最初に聞こえてくる英文に対する応答として最も適切なものを A ～ C の中から 48
選びましょう。

3. A   B   C

4. A   B   C

Part III SHORT CONVERSATIONS

会話を聞き、下の英文が会話の内容と合っていれば T（True）、間違っていれば 49
F（False）を○で囲みましょう。

5. The man is having difficulty reading the map.　　　　　T　　F

6. The man tells the woman not to miss her train.　　　　　T　　F

LET'S READ ALOUD & WRITE!

音読筆写で覚えよう！

授業のまとめとして、今日学習した対話文を３回書き写して
しっかり覚えましょう。１度英文を声に出して読んでから書き
写すと頭に残りやすくなります。

今日のまとめ

英語で答えられますか？　　　Do you enjoy visiting museums?

UNIT 09

What do you want me to do?

タカシとマーサは部室で話をしています。マーサはとても困っているようです。会話では、問題点を述べたり、依頼したりする際の表現を学びます。また、文法では**不定詞**に焦点を当てて学習します。

 **WARM-UP** 　　授業前に確認しておこう！

Vocabulary Preview

1 ～ 10 の語句の意味として適切なものを a ～ j の中から選びましょう。　🎵 CD 50

1. anytime	_____	a.	外国の
2. character	_____	b.	悪い、間違って
3. schedule	_____	c.	完成した
4. finished	_____	d.	～を完成させる
5. foreign	_____	e.	ほとんど
6. complete (v.)	_____	f.	どういたしまして、いつでも
7. presentation	_____	g.	～を（…に）予定する
8. almost	_____	h.	文字
9. take	_____	i.	発表
10. wrong	_____	j.	（時間が）かかる

[Note] v.: = verb（動詞）

ビートに乗って 1 ～ 10 の語句を発音してみましょう。

Grammar Point 不定詞

It's difficult **to make** a presentation in English.

　　　　　　　　　　　（英語でプレゼンをするのは難しいです）

I'm sorry **to trouble** you, but can I talk to you for a minute?

　　　　　　　　　　　（邪魔してすみませんが、少し話をしてもいいですか？）

I have lots of homework **to do** today.

　　　　　　　　　　　（今日はしなければならない宿題がたくさんあります）

　≪ to ＋動詞の原形≫の形を **to 不定詞**または単に**不定詞**と呼びますが、その用法は下の表のように大きく 3 つに分けられます。

名詞的用法	～すること	I want **to experience** a homestay.
副詞的用法	～するために（目的）	Martha is saving money **to buy** a car.
	～して（感情の原因）	We're very happy **to hear** that.
形容詞的用法	～すべき	I have something **to tell** you. ←

> 形容詞的用法は名詞のすぐ後ろにきてその名詞を説明します。「話すべき何かを持っている」→「話がある」

54

また、下の表のように、to 不定詞の前に what や how などの疑問詞がついてまとまった意味を表す他、enough ... to ... や too ... to ... といった慣用表現もあります。例文の日本語訳を完成させながら使い方を確認しましょう。

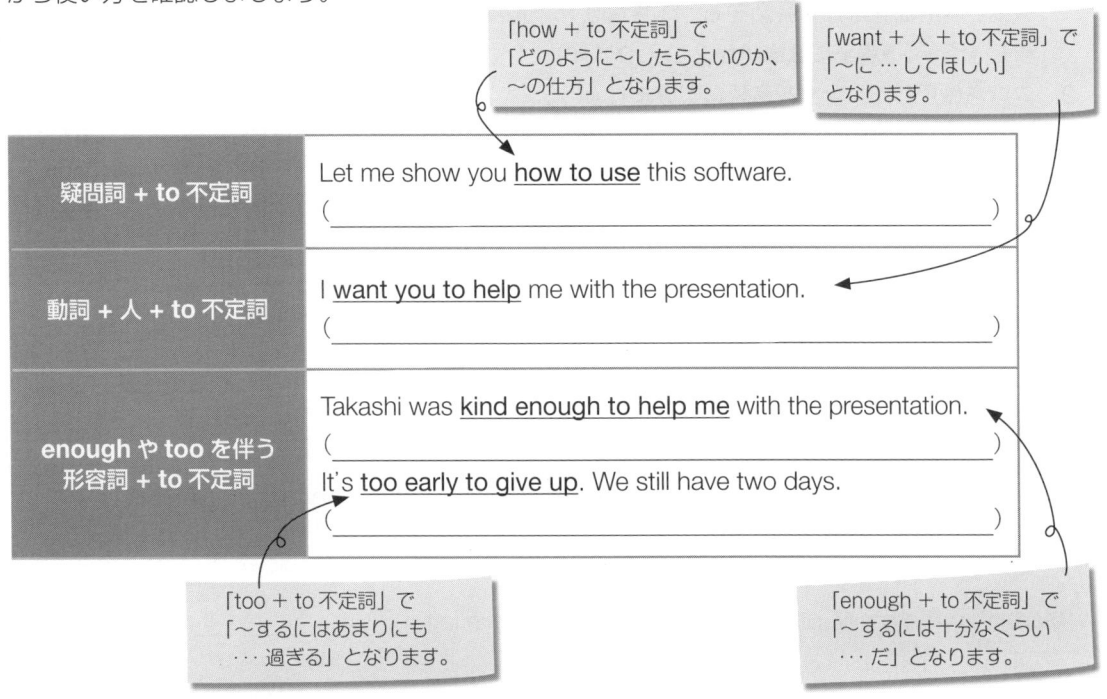

疑問詞 + **to** 不定詞	Let me show you <u>how to use</u> this software. (　　　　　　　　　　　　　　　　　　　　　)
動詞 + 人 + **to** 不定詞	I <u>want you to help</u> me with the presentation. (　　　　　　　　　　　　　　　　　　　　　)
enough や **too** を伴う 形容詞 + **to** 不定詞	Takashi was <u>kind enough to help me</u> with the presentation. (　　　　　　　　　　　　　　　　　　　　　) It's <u>too early to give up</u>. We still have two days. (　　　　　　　　　　　　　　　　　　　　　)

「how + to 不定詞」で「どのように〜したらよいのか、〜の仕方」となります。

「want + 人 + to 不定詞」で「〜に …してほしい」となります。

「too + to 不定詞」で「〜するにはあまりにも… 過ぎる」となります。

「enough + to 不定詞」で「〜するには十分なくらい… だ」となります。

 LET'S LISTEN!

会話の大意を聞き取ろう！

タカシとマーサの会話を聞いて、質問に対する答えとして最も適切なものを A ～ C の中から 1 つ選びましょう。　 51

Question 1 How does Martha find preparing for her presentation?

A. It's difficult.
B. It's exciting.
C. It's interesting.

Question 2 When is Martha's presentation scheduled?

A. Tomorrow
B. This Wednesday
C. Next week, on Wednesday

Question 3 What does Martha ask Takashi to do?

A. Help her make slides
B. Help her read kanji
C. Listen to her presentation

LET'S CHECK & READ ALOUD! 音読してみよう！

1. スクリプトを見ながら会話をもう１度聞き、下線部に当てはまる表現を書き入れましょう。（下線部には単語が２つ入ります） 51
2. 内容を確認して、全文を音読してみましょう。
3. タカシとマーサの役割をパートナーと一緒に演じてみましょう。

Let's Practice the Roleplay!

Takashi's Role   Martha's Role

Takashi and Martha talk at the clubroom.

| Takashi | Hello, Martha. Is ①_____? You look really tired. |

| Martha | Hello, Takashi. Everything is fine. I'm just ②_____ preparing for my presentation in Japanese. |

| Takashi | It's never easy to make a presentation in a foreign language. When is ③_____? |

| Martha | It's on Wednesday. I have only two days left ④_____ it. |

| Takashi | Don't worry. I have nothing to do now, so I can help you. |

| Martha | Thanks. That's very ⑤_____ you. |

| Takashi | Anytime. So, what do you want me to do? |

| Martha | My slides are ⑥_____ now, so could you tell me how to say these words? |

| Takashi | Sure. I can do that. |

| Martha | Thank you. Chinese characters are very difficult ⑦_____, and it takes a lot of time to ⑧_____ all in the dictionary. |

♪♪ **聞き取りのヒント** ♪♪

単語の中には通常はっきりと発音されず聞き取りにくいものがあります。前置詞、接続詞、冠詞、人称代名詞などは、文法的な機能が主であるため**機能語**と呼ばれ、その発音は通常弱くなります。例えば、to は「トゥー」[túː] ではなく、「トゥ」[tu] や「タ」[tə]、of は「オヴ」[ɔ́v] ではなく「ァヴ」[əv] や「ヴ」[v] のようにしか聞こえません。こうした発音にも慣れておきましょう。

 **GRAMMAR**

A. 例にならい、カッコ内に to が必要であれば to を、不要であれば×を書き入れましょう。

> 例 I have lots of reports (*to*) make.

1. I'd like (　　　　　) something to eat.
2. I'd like (　　　　　) pay by credit card.
3. Our coach makes us (　　　　　) practice hard.
4. Our coach tells us (　　　　　) practice hard.

B. 例にならい、枠の中から適切な単語を選び、to不定詞の形にして次の1〜4の文を完成させましょう。

> 例 I have a lot of work (*to do*).

1. I need a good coffee shop (　　　　　　　) at.
2. Good (　　　　　　) you again. How are things going?
3. Jenny has no desire (　　　　　　) rich.
4. I need someone (　　　　　　) care of my dog during my trip.

> do ✓
> study
> see
> take
> become

C. 日本語の意味に合うようにカッコ内の語句を並べ替え、英文を完成させましょう。ただし、文の始めにくる単語も小文字にしてあり、1つ余分な語句が含まれています。

1. 宿題を明日提出してもよろしいですか？

(hand in / it / you / would / be possible / to) the homework tomorrow?

_____

2. 今日はとても疲れているので勉強できません。

(to / I'm / study / tired / enough / too) tonight.

_____

3. 質問があったら気軽に聞いてください。

(feel / me / free / asking / ask / to) if you have any questions.

_____

4. どの授業を取るべきか教えてください。

Please tell (take / class / whether / to / me / which).

_____

次のパッセージを読んで1～3の質問に答えましょう。 52

Fraternities and Sororities

For some American students, joining a fraternity or a sorority is an important part of their campus life. A fraternity is a group of male students, while a sorority is a group of female students. New members of these single-sex societies often have to pass difficult entrance tests. They also use special symbols and passwords to maintain their group identity and privacy. For example, they use Greek letters, such as sigma and delta. They sometimes do charity work and can provide leadership skills. But they also have a dark side. Many people complain that their elitist ideas and hard drinking create an unhealthy environment for students.

1. A fraternity is a group of men _____.

   A. and women

   B. with no girlfriends

   C. with shared interests

2. Fraternities and sororities try to keep many of their activities _____.

   A. in darkness

   B. private

   C. public

3. Fraternities and sororities are known as "Greek societies" because they _____.

   A. began in ancient Athens

   B. speak the Greek language to each other

   C. use Greek letters for their names

sigma

delta

 NOTES

society: 団体   identity: 独自性
Greek letter: ギリシャ文字   elitist: エリート主義の

 **CHALLENGE YOURSELF!**

Part Ⅰ PHOTOGRAPHS

A ～ C の英文を聞き、写真の描写として最も適切なものを選びましょう。　🎧 53

1.

A　　B　　C

2.

A　　B　　C

Part Ⅱ QUESTION-RESPONSE

最初に聞こえてくる英文に対する応答として最も適切なものを A ～ C の中から　🎧 54
選びましょう。

3.　A　　B　　C

4.　A　　B　　C

Part Ⅲ SHORT CONVERSATIONS

会話を聞き、下の英文が会話の内容と合っていれば T（True）、間違っていれば　🎧 55
F（False）を○で囲みましょう。

5. The man asks the woman what time it is.　　　　T　　　F

6. The man has made a mistake with the homework deadline.　　T　　　F

LET'S READ ALOUD & WRITE!

授業のまとめとして、今日学習した対話文を 3 回書き写して
しっかり覚えましょう。1 度英文を声に出して読んでから書き
写すと頭に残りやすくなります。

今日のまとめ

英語で答えられますか？　　　Have you ever made a presentation in English?

10 I'm on a tight budget.

文法 **関係詞**

マーサとジェニーは学生食堂でお金のやりくりについて話をしています。会話では、理由を述べたり、理解を示したりする際の表現を学びます。また、文法では<u>関係詞</u>に焦点を当てて学習します。

 WARM-UP　　　　　　　　　　　　　　授業前に確認しておこう！

Vocabulary Preview

1～10の語句の意味として適切なものをa～jの中から選びましょう。　　🎵 56

1. actually	_____	a.	理想的な
2. special	_____	b.	特別な
3. barely	_____	c.	食料品
4. expensive	_____	d.	かろうじて
5. grocery	_____	e.	実際
6. opening	_____	f.	（仕事の）空き、就職口
7. rent	_____	g.	高価な
8. tight	_____	h.	厳しい
9. cover	_____	i.	（費用などを）まかなう
10. ideal	_____	j.	家賃

ビートに乗って1～10の語句を発音してみましょう。

Grammar Point 関係詞

We need <u>a new member</u> **who** can play the drums.

（私たちはドラムを演奏できる新しいメンバーを必要としています）

I have <u>a friend</u> **whose** father teaches at this school.

（私には父親がこの学校で教師をしている友人がいます）

I've lost <u>the picture</u> **that** Martha gave me.

（私はマーサがくれた写真をなくしてしまいました）

　「ドラムを演奏できる新しいメンバー」のように、下線部分と名詞（この場合は「メンバー」）をつなぐ（関係づける）働きをするのが**関係代名詞**です。関係代名詞で説明される名詞を**先行詞**と呼びますが、その先行詞が人かそうでないかによって関係代名詞は次の表のような使い分けをします。

先行詞	主格	所有格	目的格
人	who	whose	who / whom
人以外	which	whose	which
人・人以外	that	—	that

 目的格の関係代名詞は省略されることもあります。

1番目の例文は次の2つの文を1つにしたものと考えればよいでしょう。

A. We need <u>a new member</u>.
B. <u>He</u> can play the drums.

➡ We need a new member <u>who</u> can play the drums.

下線部分の a new member と he は同一人物なのでここを関係代名詞でつなぐわけですが、he は元の文の主語なので主格の関係代名詞 who を使います。同様に、3番目の例文は次の2文を1つにしたものです。下線部分の a picture と it が同一のものなのでここを関係代名詞でつなぎ、it は元の文の目的語なので目的格の関係代名詞 that（もしくは which）を使います。

A. Martha gave me <u>a picture</u>.
B. I've lost <u>it</u>.

➡ I've lost the picture <u>that</u> Martha gave me.

下の例文の日本語訳を完成させながら使い方を確認しましょう。

A quiz is a short test <u>that</u> a teacher gives to a class.

(_____)

A handout is a document <u>that</u> is given to students in class.

(_____)

 ## LET'S LISTEN!

会話の大意を聞き取ろう！

マーサとジェニーの会話を聞いて、質問に対する答えとして最も適切なものを A ～ C の中から1つ選びましょう。 57

Question 1 How does Martha feel about her new phone?

A. It was too expensive.
B. She likes it very much.
C. It's very easy to use.

Question 2 What is Jenny saving money for?

A. A party
B. A new phone
C. A trip

Question 3 What does Martha suggest?

A. Jenny should work part-time.
B. Jenny should spend less money.
C. Jenny should take Japanese lessons.

LET'S CHECK & READ ALOUD! 音読してみよう！

1. スクリプトを見ながら会話をもう1度聞き、下線部に当てはまる表現を書き入れ
   ましょう。（下線部には単語が2つ入ります）   57
2. 内容を確認して、全文を音読してみましょう。
3. マーサとジェニーの役割をパートナーと一緒に演じてみましょう。

Let's Practice the Roleplay!

Jenny's Role　　Martha's Role

Jenny and Martha talk at the school cafeteria.

Jenny	Hey, Martha. Is this the new iPhone?
Martha	Yes, I bought it last week. It ①_____, but I like it very much.
Jenny	It's nice. I'd like a new phone, but I'm on a ②_____. I need to save as much money as I can before summer.
Martha	Are you saving for something special?
Jenny	Yes, it's for a trip ③_____ planning. In fact, I ④_____ enough money to ⑤_____ and cover my rent this month.
Martha	That's too bad. Look, there's ⑥_____ at the restaurant where I work. Why don't you work there?
Jenny	That's a good idea. But my Japanese still isn't good enough.
Martha	Don't worry. They need someone ⑦_____ speak English.
Jenny	Really? Then I think I'll try it. Tell me more about the job.
Martha	Sure. Actually, ⑧_____ for the position.

♪ 聞き取りのヒント ♪

会話の中で使われていた that I'm は、「ザット・アイム」ではなく、「ザッタイム」のように聞こえます。
これがアメリカ英語になると、[t] が母音に挟まれた場合、ラ行に近い音になりますので、「ザッラ
イム」のように聞こえます。better [bétər] なども、アメリカ人が発音すると「ベター」ではなく「ベ
ラー」のように聞こえることがあります。

 **GRAMMAR**

A. 次の文の空所に補うのに適切な関係代名詞をカッコ内から選び○で囲みましょう。

1. I have a friend (who / whose / which) can speak both German and French.

2. I have a friend (who / whose / that) brother is a professional baseball player.

3. A document (who / whose / that) is given to students in class is called a handout.

4. That's not (what / which / that) I need.

B. 例にならい、関係代名詞節を用いて2つの文を1つにまとめましょう。出だしが書いてあるものはそれに続く形で文を作りましょう。

例　Martha gave me a picture. I've lost it.

　　I've lost the picture (that) Martha gave me.

1. The blog is very useful. You told me about it.

The blog _____

2. This is the new iPhone. I bought it yesterday.

This is _____

3. I have a friend. Her father is a popular singer.

_____

4. Martha is talking to a man. Do you know him?

_____

C. 日本語の意味に合うようにカッコ内の語句を並べ替え、英文を完成させましょう。ただし、文の始めにくる単語も小文字にしてあり、1つ余分な語句が含まれています。

1. 先週オープンしたその喫茶店はとても人気があります。

(last week / which / coffee shop / the / who / opened) is very popular.

_____

2. あそこに立っている女性がベイカー先生です。

(which / is / standing / over there / who / the woman) is Ms. Baker.

_____

3. 60点未満だった学生はテストを再受験しなければなりません。

Students (scores / below / who / 60 / were / whose) must take the test again.

_____

4. 君が教えてくれた場所に行きました。

(the place / I / who / told me about / you / went to).

_____

 **LET'S READ!**

次のパッセージを読んで 1 〜 3 の質問に答えましょう。 58

Applying to College in the U.S.

College entry in the U.S. is a little different from that in Japan. In Japan, <u>college applicants</u> take an entrance examination on one specific day, but not in the U.S. Instead, they provide their high school grades and SAT scores in reading, writing and math. They also fill out the college's application form, write an admission essay, and may need to provide a letter of recommendation. If the college is interested in the application, it may invite the student for an interview. If the interview goes well, the student will receive an acceptance letter from the college.

1. The underlined phrase "college applicants" means _____.

   A. students who study at a college

   B. students who have been accepted by a college

   C. students who request a place to study in a college

2. After providing all the important documents, a student may be asked to _____.

   A. attend an interview

   B. fill out an application form

   C. send an acceptance letter

3. A letter of recommendation is usually written by the _____.

   A. student

   B. student's high school teacher

   C. college

 **NOTES**

specific: 特定の   application form: 出願書類

admission essay: 志望理由書   acceptance letter: 合格通知

Part I PHOTOGRAPHS

A～Cの英文を聞き、写真の描写として最も適切なものを選びましょう。

 59

1.

A   B   C

2.

A   B   C

Part II QUESTION-RESPONSE

最初に聞こえてくる英文に対する応答として最も適切なものをA～Cの中から
選びましょう。

 60

3. A   B   C

4. A   B   C

Part III SHORT CONVERSATIONS

会話を聞き、下の英文が会話の内容と合っていればT（True）、間違っていれば
F（False）を○で囲みましょう。

61

5. The man's new jacket was very expensive.   T   F

6. The man has found a new part-time job.   T   F

LET'S READ ALOUD & WRITE! 音読筆写で覚えよう！

授業のまとめとして、今日学習した対話文を3回書き写して
しっかり覚えましょう。1度英文を声に出して読んでから書き
写すと頭に残りやすくなります。

 今日のまとめ

英語で答えられますか？　　　Are you on a tight budget?

What do you think of this program?

文法　形容詞・副詞

タカシは学生食堂でキャシー先生に話しかけます。相談したいことがあるようです。会話では、意見を尋ねたり、励ましたりする際の表現を学びます。また、文法では**形容詞・副詞**に焦点を当てて学習します。

 WARM-UP

授業前に確認しておこう！

Vocabulary Preview

1 ～ 10 の語句の意味として適切なものを a ～ j の中から選びましょう。　🎵 62

1. abroad	_____	a. 経験
2. advice	_____	b. その上、さらに
3. besides	_____	c. 文化
4. culture	_____	d. 少しの間
5. definitely	_____	e. 緊張した
6. experience	_____	f. 助言
7. for a minute	_____	g. 海外に、外国へ
8. natural	_____	h. 自然の、もっともな
9. nervous	_____	i. まったくその通りだ
10. regret	_____	j. ～を後悔する

ビートに乗って 1 ～ 10 の語句を発音してみましょう。

Grammar Point 形容詞・副詞

That was a very **easy** test.

（あれはとても簡単なテストでした）［形容詞］

I **barely** passed the test.

（私はかろうじてそのテストに合格しました）［副詞］

　形容詞は、1 番目の例文における easy のように、**名詞と結びついて人やものの状態や性質を説明するもの**です。形容詞は名詞の直前に置かれる他、"The test was easy." のように、動詞の後に置いて主語（＝名詞・代名詞）に説明を加えたりします。それに対し、**副詞**は、2 番目の例文における barely のように、動詞や形容詞、他の副詞といった**名詞以外のものと結びついて様子や場所、時、頻度などを説明するもの**です。次の表で副詞の種類を確認しましょう。

「様態」（どのように）を表す	well, fast など	You speak Japanese very <u>well</u>.
「場所」（どこで）を表す	here, home など	We came <u>home</u> late last night.
「時」（いつ）を表す	late, soon など	I hope you'll get well <u>soon</u>.
「頻度」 （どれくらいの度合いで） を表す	always, often, usually, never など	I <u>usually</u> walk to school, but today I took the bus. Martha is <u>never</u> late for class.
「程度」（どれだけ）を表す	almost, hardly など	I <u>almost</u> forgot.

一般動詞の前、
be 動詞・助動詞の
後に置くのが基本。

修飾する語句の直前が基本。ただし
動詞を修飾する場合は一般動詞の前、
be 動詞・助動詞の後に置きます。

　一般に、副詞は carefully や easily のように –ly で終わるものが多いですが、hard（懸命に、激しく）と hardly（ほとんど～でない）、late（遅れて）と lately（最近）のように、似た副詞で意味の異なるものがあります。また、形容詞に関しても、few と a few や little と a little など、a の有無で意味が異なるものがあり要注意です。

　下の例文の日本語訳を完成させながら使い方を確認しましょう。

a few は「（数について）
少しはある」、few は「（数
について）ほとんどない」
となります。

It was raining so <u>hard</u> that we could <u>hardly</u> see anything.

(_____)

I need <u>a few</u> hours to finish this homework.

(_____)

a little は「（量について）
少しはある」、little は
「（量について）ほとんど
ない」となります。

We have <u>little</u> time today, so let's discuss it tomorrow.

(_____)

① LET'S LISTEN!

会話の大意を聞き取ろう！

タカシとキャシー先生の会話を聞いて、質問に対する答えとして最も適切なものを
A ～ C の中から 1 つ選びましょう。

 63

Question 1 Has Takashi ever been abroad?

　A. Yes, a few times.

　B. Yes, but only once.

　C. No, he hasn't.

Question 2 How does Takashi feel about the program?

　A. Excited

　B. Worried

　C. Surprised

Question 3 What does Cathy suggest at the end of the conversation?

　A. Takashi should take part in the program.

　B. Takashi should study English harder.

　C. Takashi should study abroad for a year.

LET'S CHECK & READ ALOUD!　　　　音読してみよう！

1. スクリプトを見ながら会話をもう１度聞き、下線部に当てはまる表現を書き入れましょう。（下線部には単語が２つ入ります） 63

2. 内容を確認して、全文を音読してみましょう。

3. タカシとキャシー先生の役割をパートナーと一緒に演じてみましょう。

Let's Practice the Roleplay!

Takashi's Role　　Cathy's Role

Takashi speaks to Cathy at the school cafeteria.

| Takashi | Cathy, can I talk to you for a minute? I ①_____ advice. |

| Cathy | Sure. How can I ②_____? |

| Takashi | What do you think of this program? It's for a summer English course. |

| Cathy | It's a great program. You can learn a lot about American culture. |

| Takashi | Yes, I think so, too. But I'm a little nervous. I've never ③_____. |

| Cathy | Well, that's ④_____. Most people would feel the same way. |

| Takashi | Besides, I don't think my English is ⑤_____. |

| Cathy | Don't worry. Your English is ⑥_____, and this overseas program would be a great experience. |

| Takashi | ⑦_____ try it? |

| Cathy | Definitely. I don't think you'll ⑧_____. |

♪ 聞き取りのヒント ♫

need your が「ニージョア」のように聞こえる**音の同化**についてはすでに触れましたが、[p] や [k] の子音で終わる単語の後に、you [júː] などのような [j] の音で始まる語が来たときも、やはり発音がわかりにくくなります。例えば、help you は「ヘルプユー」ではなく「ヘルピュ」、take you は「テイクユー」ではなく「テイキュ」のように、日本語の拗音（「キャ」などの小さなゃ）に似た音になります。

 **GRAMMAR**

文法に強くなろう！

A. 例にならい、枠の中から適切な単語を選んで次の1〜4の文を完成させましょう。

例　You speak Japanese very (*well*) .

1. My score was below average, and I (　　　　　) passed the test.
2. This room isn't big (　　　　　) for a party.
3. How (　　　　　) can you finish the homework?
4. My shift (　　　　　) starts at seven, but today I started at six.

> enough
> usually
> soon
> well ✓
> barely

B. 例にならい、カッコ内から正しい語句を選び○で囲みましょう。

例　Cathy is a very ((safe) / safely) driver.

1. You're really (well / good) at karaoke.
2. You look (sad / sadly) . What's wrong?
3. Be (quiet / quietly)! I'm talking on the phone now.
4. Don't worry. Jeff will drive me (to home / home) .

C. 日本語の意味に合うようにカッコ内の語句を並べ替え、英文を完成させましょう。ただし、文の始めにくる単語も小文字にしてあり、1つ余分な語句が含まれています。

1. 食堂に人はほとんどいませんでした。

(there / people / in / few / a few / were) the cafeteria.

_____

2. 少し1人になりたいのです。

(need / time / a little / a few / I / alone) .

_____

3. 何か冷たい飲み物はありますか？

(something / is / to / there / are / cold) drink?

_____

4. 私たちは週末が待ち遠しいです。

We can (wait / the / weekend / hard / hardly / till) .

_____

次のパッセージを読んで１〜３の質問に答えましょう。 64

University Entrance in Britain

Few British universities have entrance examinations. Admission is decided by a student's grades in the national examinations called "A-Levels." In their final year of high school, students choose a university course and fill in an application form. They write a personal essay and get a reference from their high school. Next, they usually have an interview with the university. If the interview goes well, the university will make an offer. For example, they might say, "We'll accept you if you get two As on your A-Level results." Students then take the A-Level tests, and if their grades are good enough, they can enter the university.

1. Students in the U.K. usually need to _____ to enter their preferred university.

   A. get good A-Level grades

   B. take an essay examination

   C. take an entrance examination

2. A-Levels are _____.

   A. a type of interview test

   B. a student's grades on a test

   C. a type of national test

3. Interviews are _____ getting a place in British universities.

   A. only a minor part of

   B. an important part of

   C. rarely required for

 NOTES

A-Levels: A レベル（高校卒業レベルに到達していることを示す学業修了認定試験で、成績
　　　　 は A*, A, B, C, D, E の６段階で示される。正式名称は一般教育修了上級レベル）

personal essay: 志望理由書　　　　　　　　reference: 推薦書

CHALLENGE YOURSELF!

リスニング力を試そう！

Part Ⅰ PHOTOGRAPHS

A 〜 C の英文を聞き、写真の描写として最も適切なものを選びましょう。 **CD** 65

1.

A　　B　　C

2.

A　　B　　C

Part Ⅱ QUESTION-RESPONSE

最初に聞こえてくる英文に対する応答として最も適切なものを A 〜 C の中から
選びましょう。 **CD** 66

3. A　　B　　C

4. A　　B　　C

Part Ⅲ SHORT CONVERSATIONS

会話を聞き、下の英文が会話の内容と合っていれば T（True）、間違っていれば
F（False）を○で囲みましょう。 **CD** 67

5. The man doesn't regret his time in Spain.　　　　　　　T　　　F

6. Carlos has no experience of feeling homesick.　　　　　T　　　F

LET'S READ ALOUD & WRITE!

音読筆写で覚えよう！

授業のまとめとして、今日学習した対話文を 3 回書き写して
しっかり覚えましょう。1 度英文を声に出して読んでから書き
写すと頭に残りやすくなります。

今日のまとめ

英語で答えられますか？　　　Do you want to take a summer English course?

I'm reviewing what I studied.

文法 接続詞・前置詞

期末試験前のある日、タカシとマーサは学生ラウンジで話をしています。会話では、近況を尋ねたり、確信を示したりする際の表現を学びます。また、文法では**接続詞・前置詞**に焦点を当てて学習します。

 WARM-UP

授業前に確認しておこう！

Vocabulary Preview

1 ～ 10 の語句の意味として適切なものを a ～ j の中から選びましょう。　　🎵 68

1. final exam	_____	a.	科目
2. not at all	_____	b.	寝ずに起きている
3. pass	_____	c.	確信して
4. positive	_____	d.	期末試験
5. required	_____	e.	まったく～でない
6. review	_____	f.	～を復習する
7. sleepy	_____	g.	～を休日にする
8. stay up	_____	h.	眠い
9. subject	_____	i.	必須の
10. take ... off	_____	j.	合格する

ビートに乗って 1 ～ 10 の語句を発音してみましょう。

Grammar Point 接続詞・前置詞

I stayed up <u>until</u> two a.m., <u>so</u> I'm very sleepy now.

（午前 2 時まで起きていたので、今とても眠いです）

I'll get there <u>as soon as</u> school is over.

（学校が終わり次第そこに行きます）

Afternoon classes were canceled <u>because of</u> heavy rain.

（大雨のために午後の授業は休講になりました）

　接続詞は様々な語や句、節などを結びつける役割を果たすものです。and や if のようによく知られたものの他、every time（～する度に）や in case（～の場合は）などのように 2 語以上で接続詞的に使われるものもあります。次の表に枠の中から適切な接続詞を書き入れて確認しましょう。

because	～なので	after	～した後で		～しなければ
or	または	before	～する前に		～だけれども
so	それで	when	～するとき		～したらすぐに
	～の間		～するまで		～である限りは

because ✓
while
although
until
as long as
unless
as soon as

次に、**前置詞**は、<u>in</u> May や <u>on</u> the desk のように、名詞や名詞句の前に置かれ、形容詞や副詞の役割を果たすものです。前置詞と名詞が一緒になったものを**前置詞句**と呼びます。

接続詞と前置詞では、while と during、because と because of など、意味の似たものがありますので違いを確認しておきましょう。接続詞と前置詞を見分けるポイントは次の通りです。

接続詞	その後に主語と動詞を含む語句（＝**節**）が続く。 ex.) Cathy canceled her class today <u>because</u> she was ill.
前置詞	その後に主語と動詞を含まない語句（＝**句**）が続く。 ex.) Cathy canceled her class today <u>because of</u> her illness.

下の例文の日本語訳を完成させながら使い方を確認しましょう。

Please turn off your phone <u>during</u> the test.

(_____)

I was very nervous <u>while</u> (I was) waiting for my exam results.

(_____)

 LET'S LISTEN! 会話の大意を聞き取ろう！

タカシとマーサの会話を聞いて、質問に対する答えとして最も適切なものを A 〜
C の中から 1 つ選びましょう。　CD 69

Question 1 What does Takashi say about the final exam?

　A. He'll take it tomorrow.

　B. He has three days left.

　C. He's not ready for it yet.

Question 2 What did Takashi do last night?

　A. He studied one of the required subjects.

　B. He stayed up talking with a friend.

　C. He did his English homework.

Question 3 What does Martha suggest?

　A. They should study together.

　B. Takashi should take a break.

　C. Takashi should study harder.

LET'S CHECK & READ ALOUD!

音読してみよう！

1. スクリプトを見ながら会話をもう1度聞き、下線部に当てはまる表現を書き入れましょう。（下線部には単語が2つ入ります）
2. 内容を確認して、全文を音読してみましょう。
3. タカシとマーサの役割をパートナーと一緒に演じてみましょう。

 69

Let's Practice the Roleplay!

Martha's Role   Takashi's Role

Martha and Takashi talk at the school lounge.

Martha　Hello, Takashi. I haven't ①＿＿＿＿＿＿＿＿ in a while! How are things?

Takashi　Hello, Martha. Not so good. I have a final exam next week, and I'm not ready ②＿＿＿＿＿＿＿＿.

Martha　You'll be fine. What are you studying right now?

Takashi　Psychology. I'm reviewing ③＿＿＿＿＿＿＿＿ studied last night. I ④＿＿＿＿＿＿＿＿ until three a.m.

Martha　Wow! You ⑤＿＿＿＿＿＿＿＿ tired.

Takashi　Yes, I'm very tired and sleepy. But I'm not sure if I'll pass.

Martha　I'm sure ⑥＿＿＿＿＿＿＿＿ pass.

Takashi　Really?

Martha　Yes, I'm positive. Why don't you take ⑦＿＿＿＿＿＿＿＿ and start again tomorrow?

Takashi　You may be right, but I can't. This is a ⑧＿＿＿＿＿＿＿＿, so I need to pass.

♪ 音読のヒント ♪♪

会話の中で使われていた "I'm sure that ..." の that のように、「～ということ」という接続詞の that は読む際に強勢を取らず、弱く [ðət] と発音します。また、ポーズを取るときはその前で取ります。例えば、"I think that it's too difficult." という文を読む際にどこかで息つぎをするとすれば、I think と that の間となります。実際には I think that の後で切ることもありますが、その場合は次に何を言おうか言葉に詰まって考えているときです。

 **GRAMMAR**

A. 例にならい、枠の中から適切な単語を選んで次の 1 ～ 4 の文を完成させましょう。

> 例　I was tired, (*so*) I went to bed early.

1. Let's wait here (　　　　　) it stops raining.
2. Hurry up, (　　　　) you'll be late.
3. I was tired, (　　　　　) I went shopping.
4. (　　　　　) I was tired, I went shopping.

> but
> or
> although
> until
> so ✓

B. 例にならい、カッコ内から正しい語句を選び○で囲みましょう。

> 例　I left home ((at) / on) six o'clock.

1. Martha was late for class (because / because of) heavy traffic.
2. We'll discuss the project (in / on) Friday afternoon.
3. I'll finish this work (by / until) seven o'clock.
4. I visited a friend of mine (during / while) my stay in Kyoto.

C. 日本語の意味に合うようにカッコ内の語句を並べ替え、英文を完成させましょう。ただし、文の始めにくる単語も小文字にしてあり、1 つ余分な語句が含まれています。

1. 私の答えが合っているかどうか自信がありません。

(sure / I'm / my answer / for / not / if) is correct.

_____

2. ジェフは宿題を終わらせるために午前 2 時まで起きていました。

(by / till / up / two a.m. / stayed / Jeff) to finish his homework.

_____

3. 私は高校以来ジェニーには会っていません。

(seen / since / I / for / Jenny / haven't) high school.

_____

4. 困ったことに、今プリンターが故障しています。

(the printer / is / isn't / how / that / the trouble) working now.

_____

次のパッセージを読んで1〜3の質問に答えましょう。 70

Cramming and Pulling an All-nighter

Studying in a panic before a test is common among students all over the world. It's known as "cramming," and no matter how much teachers advise against it, many students do it. Some will even stay awake all night to study for a test. Not a good idea! Research has shown that students who lose sleep to study for tests, have more problems the next day. Not sleeping has a negative impact on your memory and the ability to connect information. It will also increase your stress levels. So get a good night's sleep before a test!

1. Teachers don't _____ studying in a panic the night before a test.

   A. avoid

   B. dislike

   C. suggest

2. Students who study all night for a test will probably _____ to concentrate.

   A. find it harder

   B. try not

   C. wake up early

3. Not sleeping well before a test causes stress levels to _____.

   A. go down

   B. go up

   C. stay the same

 NOTES

cram: 詰め込み勉強をする   stay awake: 寝ずに起きている
research: 研究

 **CHALLENGE YOURSELF!**　　　　　リスニング力を試そう！

Part Ⅰ PHOTOGRAPHS

A〜Cの英文を聞き、写真の描写として最も適切なものを選びましょう。 71

1.

　　　　A　　B　　C

2.

　　　　A　　B　　C

Part Ⅱ QUESTION-RESPONSE

最初に聞こえてくる英文に対する応答として最も適切なものをA〜Cの中から
選びましょう。 71 72

3.　A　　B　　C

4.　A　　B　　C

Part Ⅲ SHORT CONVERSATIONS

会話を聞き、下の英文が会話の内容と合っていれば T（True）、間違っていれば
F（False）を○で囲みましょう。 73

5.　The man has already finished his final exams.　　　　T　　F

6.　The man offers to help the woman with her test.　　　T　　F

LET'S READ ALOUD & WRITE!　　　　音読筆写で覚えよう！

授業のまとめとして、今日学習した対話文を3回書き写して
しっかり覚えましょう。1度英文を声に出して読んでから書き
写すと頭に残りやすくなります。

今日のまとめ

英語で答えられますか？　　　Are you quite sure that you'll pass this subject?

Final exam week is so stressful!

文法　動名詞

期末試験中のある日、タカシとマーサは大学の正門近くで話をしています。会話では、賛同したり、不安を示したりする際の表現を学びます。また、文法では**動名詞**に焦点を当てて学習します。

 WARM-UP　　　　　　　　　　　授業前に確認しておこう！

Vocabulary Preview

1 〜 10 の語句の意味として適切なものを a 〜 j の中から選びましょう。🎵 74

1. advanced	_____	a.	少なくとも
2. at least	_____	b.	〜の前で
3. bit	_____	c.	上級の
4. worried	_____	d.	くつろぐ
5. each	_____	e.	各自、おのおの
6. in front of	_____	f.	同意する
7. over	_____	g.	少し、わずか
8. relax	_____	h.	精神的に疲れる、緊張が多い
9. stressful	_____	i.	終わって
10. agree	_____	j.	心配して

ビートに乗って 1 〜 10 の語句を発音してみましょう。

Grammar Point　動名詞

　　　<u>Learning</u> a language is not just <u>**memorizing**</u> words.

　　　　　　　（言葉を学ぶとは、単に単語を覚えることではありません）[主語や補語になる]

　　I enjoy <u>**posting**</u> photos on Instagram.

　　　　　　　（私はインスタグラムに写真を投稿するのを楽しんでいます）[動詞の目的語になる]

　　I'm sorry for <u>**being**</u> late.　　　　　　　（遅刻してすみません）[前置詞の目的語になる]

　動詞の ing 形は「〜している」という進行形で使われますが、それとは別に「〜すること」のように動詞を名詞化する場合にも使われ、これを**動名詞**と言います。動詞が名詞の働きをするものには to 不定詞もありますが、3 番目の例文のように前置詞の後には to 不定詞ではなく必ず動名詞を使います。この他にも動名詞と to 不定詞には注意すべき用法がありますので、次の表で確認しましょう。

必ず動名詞を目的語とする動詞	enjoy, finish, mind, stop, suggest, etc.
必ず **to** 不定詞を目的語とする動詞	expect, hope, learn, mean, want, etc.
どちらも目的語とする動詞	begin, like, love, start, etc.

動名詞か **to** 不定詞で 意味が異なる動詞	forget, remember, try etc. 動名詞は「すでに起きたこと」、to 不定詞は「これから先のこと」と覚えておくとよいでしょう。 ex.) I <u>remember returning</u> the book to the library. （〜したことを覚えている） <u>Remember to return</u> the book to the library. （忘れずに〜する）

また、下の表に挙げる表現では動名詞がよく使われます。

be used to ...	〜に慣れている
feel like ...	〜したい気がする
How about ...?	〜してはどうですか？
Would you mind ...?	〜していただけませんか？

下の例文の日本語訳を完成させながら使い方を確認しましょう。

<u>Studying</u> abroad is a good way to learn a foreign language.

(_____)

I'm still not used to <u>speaking</u> in front of people.

(_____)

I'm studying right now. Would you mind <u>turning</u> down the music?

(_____)

 ## LET'S LISTEN! 会話の大意を聞き取ろう！

タカシとマーサの会話を聞いて、質問に対する答えとして最も適切なものを A 〜
C の中から 1 つ選びましょう。 75

Question 1 What does Martha say about her test?

A. Her score needs to be more than 70 percent.

B. She has to take it tomorrow.

C. She received the result two days ago.

Question 2 What does Takashi say about his test?

A. It's already over.

B. He's preparing for his speech.

C. Everyone has to make a speech.

Question 3 What does Martha suggest?

A. They should have lunch together.

B. They should have some ice cream.

C. They should have some coffee.

LET'S CHECK & READ ALOUD!　　　音読してみよう！

1. スクリプトを見ながら会話をもう１度聞き、下線部に当てはまる表現を書き入れ 75
   ましょう。（下線部には単語が２つ入ります）
2. 内容を確認して、全文を音読してみましょう。
3. タカシとマーサの役割をパートナーと一緒に演じてみましょう。

Let's Practice the Roleplay!

Martha's Role　　Takashi's Role

Martha and Takashi talk near the school entrance.

| Martha | Final exam week is ①_____! |

| Takashi | Yes, it ②_____. |

| Martha | I took my advanced Japanese final exam two days ago. If I don't get over 70 percent, I ③_____ the class. So I'm really worried. |

| Takashi | Well, ④_____ it's over. I'm worried about my English class tomorrow. |

| Martha | Why? Your English is excellent. |

| Takashi | Thanks. But ⑤_____ us has to make a speech to the class. I'm not good at speaking in front of a lot of people. I ⑥_____. |

| Martha | Don't worry. You'll be just fine. |

| Takashi | Thank you. That's very kind of you. |

| Martha | You know, we ⑦_____ a little bit. How about having some ice cream? |

| Takashi | I ⑧_____ more. Let's go. |

♪ 音読のヒント ♪

will not の短縮形 won't [wóunt]「ウォウント」は、want [wánt/wɔ́nt]「ワント／ウォント」と発音が似ており、区別が難しいものです。won't を発音する際は [ou] の部分を少し強調するようにすればよいでしょう。また、すでに触れたように won't など否定を表す語は、一般に文の中で強勢を入れて<u>強く、はっきりと、長めに</u>発音されますのでその点にも注意しましょう。

 **GRAMMAR**

A. 例にならい、枠の中から適切な単語を選び、動名詞か to 不定詞にして次の1〜4の文を完成させましょう。

> 例　Thank you for (*helping*) me.

> 1. I'm not good at (　　　　　) photos.
> 2. Julia wants (　　　　) Paris someday.
> 3. I'm thinking about (　　　　　) abroad.
> 4. How about (　　　　) the tennis club?

> take
> join
> study
> visit
> help ✓

B. 例にならい、カッコ内から正しい語句を選び○で囲みましょう。

> 例　I'm sorry for (be /(being)) late.

> 1. We hope (to see / seeing) you again.
> 2. I can't stand (to do / doing) homework.
> 3. You need to learn (to pace / pacing) yourself.
> 4. We practice (to read / reading) English aloud every day.

C. 日本語の意味に合うようにカッコ内の語句を並べ替え、英文を完成させましょう。ただし、文の始めにくる単語も小文字にしてあり、1つ余分な語句が含まれています。

> 1. パソコンの電源を忘れずに切ってください。
>
>   (computer / the / don't / to turn off / turning off / forget).
>
>   _____
>
> 2. 私はロンドンを訪れたことを決して忘れません。
>
>   (forget / to visit / never / visiting / London / I'll).
>
>   _____
>
> 3. 私は英語で話すことにだんだん慣れてきたところです。
>
>   (I'm / to / getting / speak / speaking / used) in English.
>
>   _____
>
> 4. 試しに1曲英語で歌ってみたらどうですか？
>
>   (try / sing / why / you / don't / singing) a song in English?
>
>   _____

次のパッセージを読んで１〜３の質問に答えましょう。　　 76

The Ivy League

You may have heard of the Ivy League. Do you know what this is?
It's a group of eight <u>highly respected</u> private universities and colleges
in the Northeastern United States, such as Princeton and Harvard. It
officially began in 1955, when these universities and colleges decided
to compete against each other in sports. But the name "Ivy League" was
first used in the 1930's. It referred to the ivy that grew on some of the
campus buildings. In those days graduating students usually planted ivy
to celebrate their graduation. If you could graduate from an Ivy League
school, it would certainly be something to celebrate.

1. The underlined phrase "highly respected" means that the Ivy League colleges and universities have a good _____.

　A. campus

　B. entrance exam

　C. reputation

2. The Ivy League had its origins in a _____ association.

　A. professional

　B. sporting

　C. working

3. Ivy is a type of _____.

　A. college building

　B. evergreen plant

　C. sporting event

 NOTES

Princeton: プリンストン大学　　　　　　　　Harvard: ハーバード大学

compete: 競う　　　　　　　　　　　　　　refer to: 〜を指す

CHALLENGE YOURSELF! リスニング力を試そう！

Part I PHOTOGRAPHS

A ～ C の英文を聞き、写真の描写として最も適切なものを選びましょう。　 77

1.

A　B　C

2.

A　B　C

Part II QUESTION-RESPONSE

最初に聞こえてくる英文に対する応答として最も適切なものを A ～ C の中から
選びましょう。

3.　A　　B　　C

4.　A　　B　　C

Part III SHORT CONVERSATIONS

会話を聞き、下の英文が会話の内容と合っていれば T（True）、間違っていれば 79
F（False）を○で囲みましょう。

5. The man has prepared well for the test.　　　　　　　　　　T　　　F

6. The man stayed up all night to study for his tests.　　　　T　　　F

LET'S READ ALOUD & WRITE! 音読筆写で覚えよう！

授業のまとめとして、今日学習した対話文を 3 回書き写して
しっかり覚えましょう。1 度英文を声に出して読んでから書き
写すと頭に残りやすくなります。

今日のまとめ

英語で答えられますか？　　　Are you good at speaking in front of a lot of people?

UNIT 14 Is this your first trip abroad?

文法 分詞

期末試験が終わった日、タカシとマーサは学生食堂で話をしています。会話では、相槌を打ったり、予定を尋ねたりする際の表現を学びます。また、文法では分詞に焦点を当てて学習します。

 WARM-UP

授業前に確認しておこう！

Vocabulary Preview

1～10 の語句の意味として適切なものを a～j の中から選びましょう。 🎵 80

1. around the corner	_____	a. ようやく、ついに
2. decide	_____	b. 決める
3. excited	_____	c. 借りる
4. exciting	_____	d.（時間を）費やす
5. finally	_____	e. 興奮して
6. hardly	_____	f. 願う
7. hope	_____	g. ほとんど～でない
8. intensive	_____	h. 興奮させるような
9. borrow	_____	i. 集中的な
10. spend	_____	j. すぐ近くに、間近に

ビートに乗って 1～10 の語句を発音してみましょう。

Grammar Point 分詞

Who is the woman talking with Cathy?

（キャシーと話している女性は誰ですか？）[現在分詞]

Books borrowed at the library need to be returned within two weeks.

（図書館で借りられた本は 2 週間以内に返却される必要があります）[過去分詞]

　分詞には**現在分詞**と**過去分詞**があり、これらは形容詞として使うことができます。上の例文のように、**現在分詞は「～している」という能動的な意味、過去分詞は「～された」という受動的な意味になります。**

　形容詞には分詞から派生しているものがあり、感情を表す動詞から派生しているものは使い分けに注意が必要です。例えば、exciting と excited はもともと動詞 excite（「（人を）興奮させる」）のそれぞれ現在分詞、過去分詞なので、exciting は「（人を）興奮させるような」という能動の意味、excited は「興奮させられた（⇒興奮した）」という受動の意味を持ちます。次の表でそうした形容詞の使い方を確認しましょう。

	物や事がどのようなものかを説明する			人がどのように感じたかを説明する	
-ing	My life is	boring. （退屈な） exciting. （刺激的な） interesting. （面白い）	-ed	I'm	bored. （退屈している） excited. （興奮している） interested. （興味を持っている）

　また、分詞の用法は下の表のように大きく３つに分けられます。
例文の日本語訳を完成させながら使い方を確認しましょう。

名詞を修飾する （限定用法）	1.I'd like some <u>iced</u> coffee. 　（ ＿＿＿＿＿＿＿＿＿＿＿ ） 2.The photos <u>taken by Martha</u> are great. 　（ ＿＿＿＿＿＿＿＿＿＿＿ ）	1語の場合は 名詞の前に 置きます。 他の語句が 加わると 名詞の後に 置きます。
補語となる （叙述用法）	3.I'm sorry. I didn't mean to <u>keep you **waiting**</u> this long. 　（ ＿＿＿＿＿＿＿＿＿＿＿ ） 4.You've <u>had your hair **cut**</u>. It looks great. 　（ ＿＿＿＿＿＿＿＿＿＿＿ ）	「keep ＋ 目的語 ＋補語」で「〈…を〉 ずっと〈…の状態 に〉しておく」と なります。 「have ＋ 目的語 ＋過去分詞」で 「〈…を〉〈…して〉 もらう、〈…〉さ れる」となります。
分詞構文※	5.<u>Seen</u> from the air, this lake is really beautiful. 　（ ＿＿＿＿＿＿＿＿＿＿＿ ）	

※分詞の導く句が副詞のように使われ、文の情報を補足します。
　「〜しながら、〜なので、〜して、〜するとき」などの意味を表します。

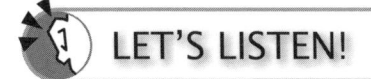 **LET'S LISTEN!**　　　　会話の大意を聞き取ろう！

タカシとマーサの会話を聞いて、質問に対する答えとして最も適切なものをА〜
Сの中から１つ選びましょう。　　 81

Question 1　Has Takashi ever been abroad?

 A. Yes, several times.

 B. Yes, but only once.

 C. No, he hasn't.

Question 2　What does Takashi say about the coming trip?

 A. He has a lot to prepare.

 B. He's almost finished his preparation.

 C. He needs to ask Cathy for advice.

Question 3　How is Martha going to spend her summer vacation?

 A. She hasn't decided yet.

 B. She's going on a trip.

 C. She's taking an intensive Japanese course.

LET'S CHECK & READ ALOUD!

音読してみよう！

1. スクリプトを見ながら会話をもう１度聞き、下線部に当てはまる表現を書き入れましょう。（下線部には単語が２つ入ります） 81

2. 内容を確認して、全文を音読してみましょう。

3. タカシとマーサの役割をパートナーと一緒に演じてみましょう。

Let's Practice the Roleplay!

Takashi's Role   Martha's Role

Takashi and Martha talk at the school cafeteria.

| Takashi | Summer vacation is just around the corner. I ①_____ wait. |

| Martha | Me, too. How will you ②_____? |

| Takashi | I'm going to join the intensive English course I talked about before. |

| Martha | Oh, that's great. I'm glad you ③_____ to do it. |

| Takashi | I asked Cathy for advice, and she said I should try it. |

| Martha | I think so, too. Is this your first ④_____? |

| Takashi | Yes, so I'm a little worried. I have a lot of things ⑤_____. |

| Martha | You worry too much. Everything will be all right. |

| Takashi | Yes, I hope so. How are you going to spend your summer vacation? |

| Martha | I'm going to ⑥_____ the country for a month. |

| Takashi | ⑦_____! |

| Martha | Yes, I'm ⑧_____. Let me show you my travel schedule. |

♪ 音読のヒント ♪

カタカナ英語が悪影響を及ぼして、vacation [veɪkéɪʃən] や great [gréɪt] を「バケーション」、「グレート」のように発音していませんか？ カタカナ英語で長音符（ー）を使っている箇所は実際の英語の発音ではそうならない場合が多いので注意しましょう。hope [hóup] や show [ʃóu] などもついつい「ホープ」や「ショー」とならないようにしましょう。

GRAMMAR

文法に強くなろう！

A. 例にならい、枠の中から適切な単語を選び、現在分詞か過去分詞にして次の1〜4の文を完成させましょう。

例 The photos (*taken*) by Martha are great.

1. The language (　　　　　) in Brazil is Portuguese.

2. We had trouble (　　　　　) a good place to eat.

3. The gate remained (　　　　　), so I couldn't enter.

4. (　　　　　) back, I really enjoyed high school.

> find
> close
> speak
> look
> take ✓

B. 例にならい、カッコ内から正しい語句を選び○で囲みましょう。

例 I'm (exciting / (excited)) about the concert on Friday.

1. Studying abroad will be an (exciting / excited) new challenge.

2. I don't want to go out with Greg. He's (boring / bored).

3. We were (shocked / shocking) at the news.

4. What kind of things are you (interesting / interested) in?

C. 日本語の意味に合うようにカッコ内の語句を並べ替え、英文を完成させましょう。ただし、文の始めにくる単語も小文字にしてあり、1つ余分な語句が含まれています。

1. 待たせてしまってすみません。

I'm (to / keep / waited / waiting / you / sorry).

_____

2. ステージで踊っている学生は私の友人です。

(dancing / the / danced / on / the stage / students) are my friends.

_____

3. 私の盗まれた自転車はまだ見つかっていません。

(bicycle / stealing / stolen / been / hasn't / my) found yet.

_____

4. 私は旅行の準備で忙しいです。

(preparing / I'm / the trip / busy / for / prepared).

_____

次のパッセージを読んで１〜３の質問に答えましょう。　　　　　　　 82

Mature Students

In Japan, most new college and university students are fresh from high school, but in the U.K. about a third of university students who start their courses are aged 21 or over. They are known as "mature" students. Many have completed high school, worked, and then decided to continue their education. Most mature students in the U.K. are aged between 21 and 24, but 10 percent are over 40. The situation is almost the same in the U.S. Adult students who are aged 22 or over are known as "nontraditional students" in American colleges and universities.

1. The underlined word "mature" means "_____".

    A. young

    B. middle-aged

    C. grown-up

2. Over _____ of students in British universities are considered to be mature students.

    A. 30 percent

    B. 40 percent

    C. 50 percent

3. The underlined phrase "nontraditional students" are students _____ in American colleges and universities.

    A. aged between 21 and 24

    B. aged 22 or over

    C. from overseas

NOTES

situation: 状況　　　　　　　　　　nontraditional: 非伝統的な

Part I PHOTOGRAPHS

A ～ C の英文を聞き、写真の描写として最も適切なものを選びましょう。　🎧 83

1.

A　　B　　C

2.

A　　B　　C

Part II QUESTION-RESPONSE

最初に聞こえてくる英文に対する応答として最も適切なものを A ～ C の中から
選びましょう。　🎧 84

3.　A　　B　　C

4.　A　　B　　C

Part III SHORT CONVERSATIONS

会話を聞き、下の英文が会話の内容と合っていれば T（True）、間違っていれば
F（False）を○で囲みましょう。　🎧 85

5. The man is feeling excited about his trip to France.　　　T　　　F

6. The woman wants to have an expensive trip.　　　T　　　F

 LET'S READ ALOUD & WRITE!　　　　音読筆写で覚えよう！

授業のまとめとして、今日学習した対話文を 3 回書き写して
しっかり覚えましょう。1 度英文を声に出して読んでから書き
写すと頭に残りやすくなります。

今日のまとめ

英語で答えられますか？　　　How are you going to spend your summer vacation?

UNIT 15
What would you like to order?

ジェニーはアルバイト先のレストランでウェイトレスとして接客します。会話では、希望を尋ねたり、注文したりする際の表現を学びます。また、文法では比較に焦点を当てて学習します。

 WARM-UP　　　　　　　　　授業前に確認しておこう！

Vocabulary Preview

1 ～ 10 の語句の意味として適切なものを a ～ j の中から選びましょう。　　CD 86

1. certainly	_____	a.	味、風味
2. dessert	_____	b.	香辛料の効いた
3. else	_____	c.	注文する
4. flavor	_____	d.	デザート
5. lobster	_____	e.	ウミザリガニ、ロブスター
6. meal	_____	f.	喉が渇いた
7. order	_____	g.	かしこまりました（客への返答）
8. recommend	_____	h.	その他の
9. spicy	_____	i.	勧める
10. thirsty	_____	j.	食事

ビートに乗って 1 ～ 10 の語句を発音してみましょう。

Grammar Point 比較

Takashi speaks English <u>as well as</u> a native speaker.

（タカシはネイティブスピーカーと同じくらい上手に英語を話します）

My mother drives <u>more carefully than</u> my father.　（母は父よりも慎重に車を運転します）

This is one of <u>the most popular</u> restaurants in Tokyo.

（ここは東京で最も人気のあるレストランの 1 つです）

　形容詞や副詞を使って「～と同じくらい…だ」と 2 つのものを比較する場合、≪as ＋形容詞／副詞＋ as...≫という形で表します。

	1 音節	2 音節	3 音節
比較級	-er		more ～
最上級	-est		most ～

　また、「～より大きい」や「最も大きい」のように、他と比較しながら話す場合、「大きい」という形容詞の<u>比較級</u>や<u>最上級</u>を使って表現します。比較級や最上級にするには、**「1 音節の短い単語は語尾に -er（比較級）、-est（最上級）をつけ、3 音節以上の長い単語は前に more（比較級）、most（最上級）をつける」**が基本ですが、2 音節の単語は両方のパターンがあります。また、不規則に変化するものも多くあります。次頁の表を完成させながら確認しましょう。

		原級	比較級	最上級	
1音節		high	higher	highest	語尾に er / est つける（基本パターン）
		large	larger	largest	語尾に r / st をつける（-e で終わる単語）
		big			子音字を重ねて er / est つける （<1母音字＋1子音字>で終わる単語）
2音節		early	earlier	earliest	y を i に変え er / est をつける （<子音字＋y>で終わる単語）
		simple	simpler	simplest	語尾に er / est つける （-er, -le, -ow で終わる単語）
		slowly ※	more slowly	most slowly	前に more / most をつける （※形容詞に -ly がついた副詞は前に 　more / most をつける）
3音節以上		difficult	more difficult	most difficult	
		many	more	most	不規則な変化をする （例外的な単語）
		good / well			
		little			
		bad			

下の例文の日本語訳を完成させながら使い方を確認しましょう。

I got my report card yesterday and my grades were **better** than high school.

(_____)

This is one of the **most popular** online games now.

(_____)

This online game is a lot of fun. If you play it once, you'll want to play it **more and more**.

(_____)

 ## LET'S LISTEN!　　　　　　　　　　　　　　　会話の大意を聞き取ろう！

ジェニーと男性客の会話を聞いて、質問に対する答えとして最も適切なものを A 〜 87
C の中から 1 つ選びましょう。

Question 1 〉 Has the customer been to this restaurant before?

  A. Yes, but only once.

  B. Yes, several times.

  C. No, this is the first time.

Question 2 〉 What does the customer want to drink?

  A. A small glass of wine

  B. A small glass of water

  C. A large glass of water

Question 3 〉 What does the customer order for dessert?

  A. Vanilla ice cream

  B. Strawberry ice cream

  C. Strawberry cake

LET'S CHECK & READ ALOUD!

音読してみよう！

1. スクリプトを見ながら会話をもう1度聞き、下線部に当てはまる表現を書き入れましょう。（下線部には単語が2つ入ります）
2. 内容を確認して、全文を音読してみましょう。
3. ジェニーとお客の役割をパートナーと一緒に演じてみましょう。

 CD 87

Let's Practice the Roleplay!

Jenny's Role　　Customer's Role

Jenny works as a server at an Italian restaurant.

Jenny	Good evening. Welcome to Marco's Italian Kitchen. What would you like ①_____?
Customer	Well, it's my first time at this restaurant. Could you ②_____?
Jenny	Of course. Our spicy lobster pasta is the most popular. I really like the roast chicken as well.
Customer	Spicy lobster pasta sounds good. I'd like that.
Jenny	Certainly. Would you like something to drink?
Customer	Oh, I'm not ③_____. I'll just have a small ④_____ water, please.
Jenny	Would you like ⑤_____ with your meal?
Customer	No, that will be all for now, thanks.
Jenny	And would you ⑥_____ any dessert?
Customer	Yes, I'd like some ice cream, please.
Jenny	⑦_____ would you like? We have vanilla and strawberry.
Customer	I'll have vanilla, please.
Jenny	I'll be ⑧_____. Let me know if you need anything else.

♪ 聞き取りのヒント ♪

すでに取り上げたように、同じ子音が連続する場合、同じ音が繰り返されるのではなく、前の子音が発音されず、その音が聞こえなくなりますから、first time は「ファースト・タイム」ではなく「ファースタイム」のように聞こえます。また、同じ子音が続く場合だけでなく、[d] と [t]、[g] と [k]、[p] と [b] など、発音の仕方の似た子音が続く場合も、前の子音ははっきり発音されず、例えば、good time は「グッタイム」、right back は「ライッバック」のように聞こえます。

 **GRAMMAR**

A. 例にならい、空所に下線部の単語の比較級か最上級を入れて次の1～4の文を完成させましょう。

　　例　I can't type very <u>fast</u>. You type (*faster*) than me.

　　1. I can't speak English very <u>well</u>. You speak it (　　　　　) than me.

　　2. The dinner was <u>expensive</u>. It was (　　　　　) than I expected.

　　3. Jenny is very <u>smart</u>. She is the (　　　　　) person I've ever met.

　　4. It was a very <u>difficult</u> test. It was the (　　　　　) test I've ever taken.

B. 例にならい、カッコ内から正しい語句を選び○で囲みましょう。

　　例　Ken is ((taller) / tallest) than Takashi.

　　1. I'm the tallest (in / from) my family.

　　2. Jeff is the tallest (in / of) all the players.

　　3. I'm a (better / best) golfer than my father.

　　4. Martha is (very / much) smarter than me.

C. 日本語の意味に合うようにカッコ内の語句を並べ替え、英文を完成させましょう。ただし、文の始めにくる単語も小文字にしてあり、1つ余分な語句が含まれています。

　　1. 第2問は第1問よりはるかに難しいです。

　　　The second question (more / than / difficult / is / better / much) the first.

　　　_____

　　2. こんなにおいしい食事をいただいたのは初めてです。

　　　This is (had / meal / best / I've ever / the / better) .

　　　_____

　　3. もう少しゆっくり話していただけませんか？

　　　(most / speak / you / slowly / more / could) ?

　　　_____

　　4. テストは思ったほど難しくありませんでした。

　　　(as / difficult / more / test / the / wasn't) as I thought.

　　　_____

 **LET'S READ!**

次のパッセージを読んで１～３の質問に答えましょう。 88

Would You Like to Take a Sandwich Course?

In Japan and the U.S. a college degree generally requires four years of study. This is also true in Britain for students studying foreign languages and technical subjects, such as engineering. Such courses include a year of study abroad or off-campus work experience, usually in the third year. They are known as "sandwich courses." Some other courses, especially those for overseas students, require an additional one-year "foundation course." However, in Britain, students on liberal arts courses begin to study their major from the first semester, so it usually only takes three years to finish their courses.

1. Students who take a sandwich course have to _____.

    A. get experience outside the university

    B. make food for other students

    C. take a special examination

2. A foundation course is designed to help students to _____.

    A. find accommodation

    B. make friends

    C. prepare for their degree course

3. Some British university degrees only take three years because students _____.

    A. are very good at studying

    B. begin their major from the first year

    C. can only afford a three-year course

NOTES

sandwich course: サンドイッチコース
　　　　　　　　（通常の３年間の学士課程に１年間の企業研修や留学をプラスし、４年
　　　　　　　　かけて学士号を取得する課程）

degree: 学位　　　　　　foundation: 基礎　　　　　liberal arts course: 文科系の課程

 **CHALLENGE YOURSELF!**　　　リスニング力を試そう！

Part I PHOTOGRAPHS

A ～ C の英文を聞き、写真の描写として最も適切なものを選びましょう。　　 89

1.

A　　B　　C

2.

A　　B　　C

Part II QUESTION-RESPONSE

最初に聞こえてくる英文に対する応答として最も適切なものを A ～ C の中から
選びましょう。　　 90

3.　A　　B　　C

4.　A　　B　　C

Part III SHORT CONVERSATIONS

会話を聞き、下の英文が会話の内容と合っていれば T（True）、間違っていれば
F（False）を○で囲みましょう。　　 91

5. The man orders food and drinks.　　　　　　　　　　T　　　F

6. The woman orders a chocolate milkshake.　　　　　T　　　F

LET'S READ ALOUD & WRITE!　　　音読筆写で覚えよう！

授業のまとめとして、今日学習した対話文を3回書き写して
しっかり覚えましょう。1度英文を声に出して読んでから書き
写すと頭に残りやすくなります。

今日のまとめ

英語で答えられますか？　　　Would you like to work at a restaurant?

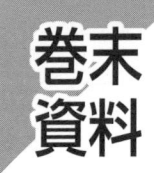

 巻末
資料

品詞の分類

名詞や動詞といった文法上の区分のことを**品詞**といい、一般に下のように分類されます。

品　詞	働　き	例
名詞（Noun）	人や物事の名前を表す。	company, sale など
冠詞（Article）	名詞の前に置かれて、その単語が特定されるものかどうかを示す。	a, an, the
代名詞（Pronoun）	名詞の代わりをする。	I, my, me, mine など
動詞（Verb）	人や物事の状態や動作を表す。	want, keep, take など
助動詞（Auxiliary verb）	動詞と組み合わせて話し手の判断を示す。	can, will, must など
形容詞（Adjective）	人や物事の性質や状態などを表す。	big, beautiful など
副詞（Adverb）	動詞や形容詞、他の副詞などを修飾する。	really, always など
前置詞（Preposition）	名詞や名詞句の前に置かれ句を作る。	of, in, under, on など
接続詞（Conjunction）	語と語、句と句、節と節をつなぐ。	and, because, or など
間投詞（Interjection）	話し手の感情を表す。	oh, wow, ouch など

　単語は必ずしも１つの品詞でしか使われないわけではありません。意味のわからない単語を辞書で引く場合も、その単語の品詞が何であるかをあらかじめ考えておくと、正しい意味に早くたどり着けるようになります。

文の要素と基本文型

英文を構成する要素には次のようなものがあります。

主　語	文の中で「〜が、〜は」に当たるもの。	名詞、代名詞
述語動詞	文の中で「〜である」や「〜する」に当たるもの。	動詞
目的語	「〜を」や「〜に」など、動作の対象を示すもの。	名詞、代名詞
補　語	主語や目的語が「どういうものか」もしくは「どんな状態なのか」を補足説明するもの。 ex. My name is Robert, but everyone calls me Bob. （私の名前はロバートですが、みんな私のことをボブと呼びます）	名詞、代名詞、形容詞
修飾語（句）	主語、述語動詞、目的語、補語に意味を付け加えるもの。 修飾語（句）を除いても文は成立します。 ex. I work for Sunrise Corporation. （私はサンライズ・コーポレーションに勤めています）	形容詞、副詞、前置詞句など

また、英文の基本文型としては下に挙げる**5 文型**がよく知られています。

第 1 文型	SV （主語 + 動詞）	I cried.（私は泣きました）
第 2 文型	SVC （主語 + 動詞 + 補語）	My name is Robert.（私の名前はロバートです）
第 3 文型	SVO （主語 + 動詞 + 目的語）	I studied economics.（私は経済学を学びました）
第 4 文型	SVO_1O_2 （主語 + 動詞 + 目的語 1 + 目的語 2）	Julia gave me the report. （ジュリアが私にその報告書をくれました）
第 5 文型	SVOC （主語 + 動詞 + 目的語 + 補語）	Everybody calls me Bob. （みんな私のことをボブと呼びます）

主語（Subject）、**述語動詞**（Verb）、**目的語**（Object）、**補語**（Complement）という基本要素の中で、目的語と補語の区別が文型を見分けるポイントになります。目的語は動詞が表す動作の対象を示し、補語は主語や目的語が「どういうものか」もしくは「どんな状態なのか」を補足説明するものです。ですから、第 2 文型と第 3 文型を見分ける場合、**「第 2 文型の場合 S = C、第 3 文型の場合 S ≠ O」**という関係に着目するとよいでしょう。また、第 4 文型と第 5 文型を見分ける場合には、**「第 4 文型の場合 $O_1 ≠ O_2$、第 5 文型の場合 O = C」**という関係が成り立つことに注意しておくことです。

人称代名詞の種類と格変化表

	数	主格 （〜は）	所有格 （〜の）	目的格 （〜に、〜を）	所有代名詞 （〜のもの）	再帰代名詞 （〜自身）
1 人称	単数	I	my	me	mine	myself
	複数	we	our	us	ours	ourselves
2 人称	単数	you	your	you	yours	yourself
	複数					yourselves
3 人称	単数	he	his	him	his	himself
		she	her	her	hers	herself
		it	its	it	—	itself
	複数	they	their	them	theirs	themselves

不規則動詞変化表

	原 形	過去形	過去分詞形	-ing 形	
A-A-A （原形、過去形、 過去分詞が すべて同じ）	cost cut hit put read	cost cut hit put read [réd]	cost cut hit put read [réd]	costing cutting hitting putting reading	（費用が）かかる 切る 叩く 置く 読む
A-B-A （原形と過去 分詞が同じ）	become come run	became came ran	become come run	becoming coming running	～になる 来る 走る
A-B-B （過去形と過去 分詞が同じ）	bring buy catch feel have hear keep leave make meet pay say spend stand teach tell think understand	brought bought caught felt had heard kept left made met paid said spent stood taught told thought understood	brought bought caught felt had heard kept left made met paid said spent stood taught told thought understood	bringing buying catching feeling having hearing keeping leaving making meeting paying saying spending standing teaching telling thinking understanding	持ってくる 買う 捕まえる 感じる 持っている 聞く 保つ 立ち去る 作る 会う 払う 言う 過ごす 立つ 教える 話す 思う 理解する
A-B-C （原形、過去形、 過去分詞が すべて異なる）	be begin break choose drink eat fall get give go know see speak take write	was/were began broke chose drank ate fell got gave went knew saw spoke took wrote	been begun broken chosen drunk eaten fallen gotten/got given gone known seen spoken taken written	being beginning breaking choosing drinking eating falling getting giving going knowing seeing speaking taking writing	～である 始まる 壊す 選ぶ 飲む 食べる 落ちる 手に入れる 与える 行く 知っている 見る 話す 取る 書く

音節

　音節とは、簡単に言うと、「母音を中心とした音のかたまり」で、[ái] といった二重母音も 1 つの母音と考えます。hot [hát] や big [bíg] などのごく短い単語は 1 音節ですが、strike [stráik] など、一見長そうに見える単語でも母音は [ái] しかありませんので、実は 1 音節です。

　単語が何音節であるかは、辞書に載っています。例えば、interesting を辞書で調べてみると、in・ter・est・ing のように区切られて表示されており、この区切りが音節の区切りを示しています。したがって、interesting は 4 音節だとわかります。

　慣れるまでは辞書で確かめるようにしてください。

発音記号の読み方① 母音編

■母音と子音

「母音」とは、日本語の「アイウエオ」のように、肺から出る空気が舌や歯、唇などに邪魔されずに自由に口から出る音のことです。これに対して、「子音」とは、喉から出る息や声が途中でいろいろと邪魔されて、口や鼻から出る音のことです。

■有声音と無声音

声帯が振動する音のことを「有声音」と言い、逆に声帯が振動しない音のことを「無声音」と言います。母音はすべて有声音ですが、子音には有声音と無声音の両方があります。

 92, 93

短母音	[ɑ]	口を思いきり開け口の奥の方から「ア」。	box / hot
	[ʌ]	口をあまり開けない「ア」。	come / bus
	[ə]	口を軽く開けて弱く「ア」。	woman / about
	[æ]	「エ」の口の形で「ア」。	bank / hand
	[i]	日本語の「イ」と「エ」の中間。	sick / it
	[i:]	唇を左右に引いて「イー」。	see / chief
	[u]	[u:]よりも少し唇をゆるめて「ウ」。	good / look
	[u:]	唇を小さく丸めて「ウー」。	school / two
	[e]	日本語の「エ」とほぼ同じ。	net / desk
	[ɔ:]	口を大きく開け唇を少し丸めて「オー」。	talk / ball
	[a:r]	口を大きく開けて「アー」の後、舌先を巻き上げた音を添える。	large / far
	[ə:r]	口を軽く開けて「アー」の後、舌先を巻き上げた音を添える。	girl / work
二重母音	[ei]	始めの音を強く発音し、後の音は軽く添える感じで、「エィ」。	game / say
	[ɔi]	上と同じ感じで、「オィ」。	boy / oil
	[ai]	上と同じ感じで、「アィ」。	write / kind
	[au]	上と同じ感じで、「アゥ」。	house / now
	[ou]	上と同じ感じで、「オゥ」。	boat / cold
	[iər]	「イァ」に舌先を巻き上げた音を添える。	dear / hear
	[eər]	「エァ」に舌先を巻き上げた音を添える。	air / bear
	[uər]	「ウァ」に舌先を巻き上げた音を添える。	poor / tour

発音記号の読み方②　子音編

CD 94~99

破裂音	[p]	「パ」行子音とほぼ同じ。	pen / cup
	[b]	[p]の有声音。「バ」行子音とほぼ同じ。	big / job
	[t]	「タ」行子音とほぼ同じ。	tea / meet
	[d]	[t]の有声音。「ダ」行子音とほぼ同じ。	day / food
	[k]	「カ」行子音とほぼ同じ。	cook / take
	[g]	[k]の有声音。「ガ」行子音とほぼ同じ。	game / leg
摩擦音	[f]	下唇を上の歯にあて、息を出して「フ」。	five / enough
	[v]	[f]の有声音で、「ヴ」。	voice / wave
	[θ]	舌先を前歯で軽く噛むようにして「ス」。	think / month
	[ð]	[θ]の有声音で、「ズ」。	there / brother
	[s]	「サ、ス、セ、ソ」の子音とほぼ同じ。	sea / nice
	[z]	[s]の有声音で、「ザ、ズ、ゼ、ゾ」の子音とほぼ同じ。	zoo / lose
	[ʃ]	「シ」とほぼ同じ。	she / fish
	[ʒ]	[ʃ]の有声音で、「ジ」。	usual / vision
	[h]	「ハー」と息を吹きかけてガラスを曇らせるときのような「ハ」。	hot / hand
破擦音	[tʃ]	「チャ」「チュ」「チョ」の子音とほぼ同じ。	church / watch
	[dʒ]	[tʃ]の有声音で、「ヂャ」「ヂュ」「ヂョ」の子音とほぼ同じ。	join / edge
鼻音	[m]	「マ」行子音とほぼ同じ。	meet / time
	[n]	舌の先を上の歯茎につけて、鼻から息を出す。	noon / run
	[ŋ]	[g]を言うつもりで、鼻から声を出す。	thing / song
側音	[l]	必ず舌の先を上の歯茎につける。	late / wall
移行音	[r]	「ウ」のように唇をすぼめる感じで、舌先は歯茎に決してつけない。	red / marry
	[w]	唇をよく丸めて発音する。	way / quick
	[j]	「ヤ、ユ、ヨ」の子音とほぼ同じ。	young / beyond

🔍 QR コードの URL 一覧

Unit 1	Takashi's Role Cathy's Role	https://youtu.be/hQ9BYVYRR7A https://youtu.be/yl9hV7V_JgA
Unit 2	Cathy's Role Takashi's Role	https://youtu.be/lwZarNtyWRI https://youtu.be/FHl-jrMur2k
Unit 3	Cathy's Role Takashi's Role Martha's Role	https://youtu.be/bbG5GqriBvQ https://youtu.be/dWqZsROdt7I https://youtu.be/egYeU7_79FM
Unit 4	Takashi's Role Martha's Role	https://youtu.be/JS9DnBxzXIo https://youtu.be/0ojcJKL1u8g
Unit 5	Martha's Role Takashi's Role	https://youtu.be/0cRtUFyoWFQ https://youtu.be/m88WxE7_Nkc
Unit 6	Martha's Role Takashi's Role	https://youtu.be/A5k7JVQbh2o https://youtu.be/NlQadPF_mtM
Unit 7	Takashi's Role Martha's Role	https://youtu.be/gDAE-IMOMpk https://youtu.be/NRRv596QiyY
Unit 8	Jenny's Role Passerby's Role	https://youtu.be/chQawt1DmvU https://youtu.be/0usnOyB-GrQ
Unit 9	Takashi's Role Martha's Role	https://youtu.be/JOjpmVjappE https://youtu.be/qH4ePmdW_7U
Unit 10	Jenny's Role Martha's Role	https://youtu.be/t6PvriQxaG4 https://youtu.be/-ETDpwTGKE8
Unit 11	Takashi's Role Cathy's Role	https://youtu.be/fQM19Z-8r2o https://youtu.be/O9M97kNPTsI
Unit 12	Martha's Role Takashi's Role	https://youtu.be/KxomOSp2DT0 https://youtu.be/iipJIH4Thik
Unit 13	Martha's Role Takashi's Role	https://youtu.be/xQgSdUOoV4o https://youtu.be/KAZiwgIdWVw
Unit 14	Takashi's Role Martha's Role	https://youtu.be/KPs8UAq4kcs https://youtu.be/2msJ6ObU9Eg
Unit 15	Jenny's Role Customer's Role	https://youtu.be/g6-sGkFhx9Q https://youtu.be/fI3jTrZaxa8

LINGUAPORTA

リンガポルタのご案内

> **リンガポルタ連動テキストをご購入の学生さんは、「リンガポルタ」を無料でご利用いただけます！**

　本テキストで学習していただく内容に準拠した問題を、オンライン学習システム「リンガポルタ」で学習していただくことができます。PCだけでなく、スマートフォンやタブレットでも学習できます。単語や文法、リスニング力などをよりしっかり身に付けていただくため、ぜひ積極的に活用してください。

　リンガポルタの利用にはアカウントとアクセスコードの登録が必要です。登録方法については下記ページにアクセスしてください。

https://www.seibido.co.jp/linguaporta/register.html

本テキスト「Let's Read Aloud & Learn English: On Campus」のアクセスコードは下記です。

7182-2043-1231-0365-0003-0060-DKSX-8297

・リンガポルタの学習機能（画像はサンプルです。また、すべてのテキストに以下の4つの機能が用意されているわけではありません）

● 多肢選択

● 空所補充（音声を使っての聞き取り問題も可能）

● 単語並びかえ（マウスや手で単語を移動）

● マッチング（マウスや手で単語を移動）

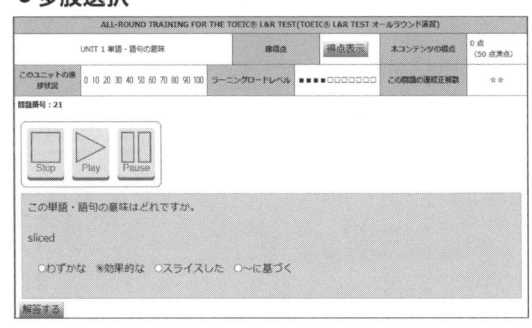

TEXT PRODUCTION STAFF

edited by　　編集
Takashi Kudo　　工藤 隆志
Minako Hagiwara　　萩原 美奈子

cover design by　　表紙デザイン
Ruben Frosali　　ルーベン・フロサリ

illustration by　　イラスト
Yoko Sekine　　関根 庸子

CD PRODUCTION STAFF

recorded by　　吹き込み者
Jack Merluzzi (AmE)　　ジャック・マルージ（アメリカ英語）
Rachel Walzer (AmE)　　レイチェル・ワルザー（アメリカ英語）
Emma Howard (BrE)　　エマ・ハワード（イギリス英語）

Let's Read Aloud & Learn English: On Campus
音読で学ぶ基礎英語《キャンパス編》

2019年1月20日　初版発行
2025年3月15日　第11刷発行

著　者　角山 照彦　Simon Capper

発行者　佐野 英一郎

発行所　株式会社 成美堂
〒101-0052　東京都千代田区神田小川町3-22
TEL 03-3291-2261　FAX 03-3293-5490
https://www.seibido.co.jp

印刷・製本　三美印刷（株）

ISBN 978-4-7919-7182-4　　　　Printed in Japan